studysync

Reading & Writing Companion

Facing Challenges

studysync.com

Copyright © BookheadEd Learning, LLC
All Rights Reserved.

Send all inquiries to:
BookheadEd Learning, LLC
610 Daniel Young Drive
Sonoma, CA 95476

Cover, ©iStock.com/aijohn784, ©iStock.com/vernonwiley, ©iStock.com/alexey_boldin, ©iStock.com/skegbydave

9 LWI 21 20 19   B

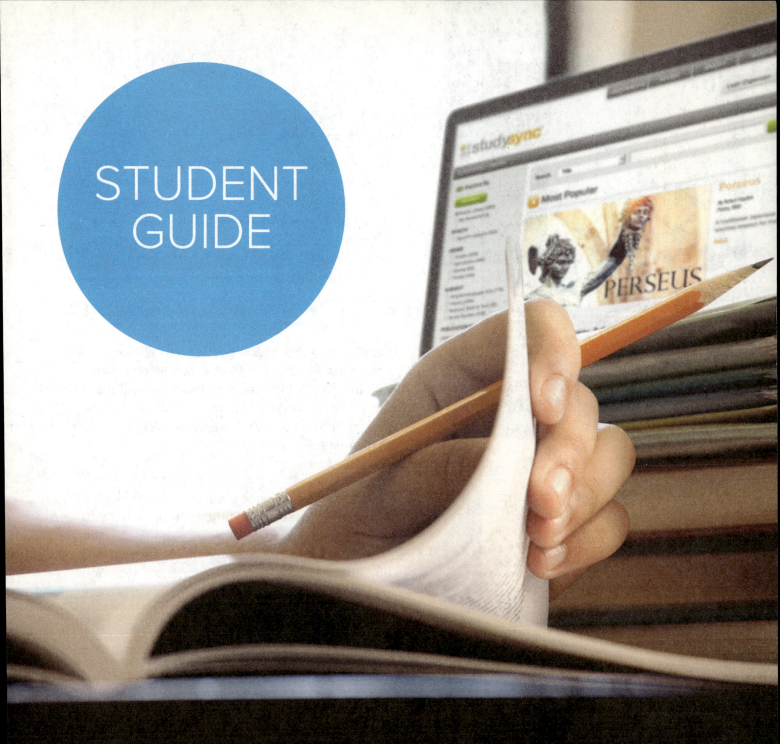

STUDENT GUIDE

GETTING STARTED

Welcome to the StudySync Reading and Writing Companion! In this booklet, you will find a collection of readings based on the theme of the unit you are studying. As you work through the readings, you will be asked to answer questions and perform a variety of tasks designed to help you closely analyze and understand each text selection. Read on for an explanation of each section of this booklet.

Student Instructions for Reading and Writing Companion

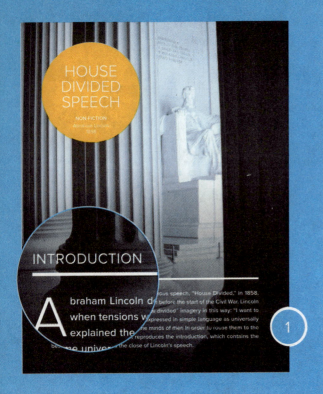

1 INTRODUCTION

An Introduction to each text provides historical context for your reading as well as information about the author. You will also learn about the genre of the excerpt and the year in which it was written.

2 FIRST READ

During your first reading of each excerpt, you should just try to get a general idea of the content and message of the reading. Don't worry if there are parts you don't understand or words that are unfamiliar to you. You'll have an opportunity later to dive deeper into the text.

Many times, while working through the Think Questions after your first read, you will be asked to **annotate** or **make annotations** about what you are reading. This means that you should use the "Notes" column to make comments or jot down any questions you may have about the text. You may also want to note any unfamiliar vocabulary words here.

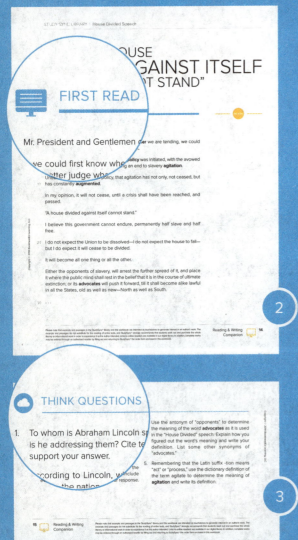

3 THINK QUESTIONS

These questions will ask you to start thinking critically about the text, asking specific questions about its purpose, and making connections to your prior knowledge and reading experiences. To answer these questions, you should go back to the text and draw upon specific evidence that you find there to support your responses. You will also begin to explore some of the more challenging vocabulary words used in the excerpt.

Reading & Writing Companion

Student Instructions for Reading and Writing Companion

 ## CLOSE READ & FOCUS QUESTIONS

After you have completed the First Read, you will then be asked to go back and read the excerpt more closely and critically. Before you begin your Close Read, you should read through the Focus Questions to get an idea of the concepts you will want to focus on during your second reading. You should work through the Focus Questions by making annotations, highlighting important concepts, and writing notes or questions in the "Notes" column. Depending on instructions from your teacher, you may need to respond online or use a separate piece of paper to start expanding on your thoughts and ideas.

 ## WRITING PROMPT

Your study of each excerpt or selection will end with a writing assignment. To complete this assignment, you should use your notes, annotations, and answers to both the Think and Focus Questions. Be sure to read the prompt carefully and address each part of it in your writing assignment.

 ## EXTENDED WRITING PROJECT

After you have read and worked through all of the unit text selections, you will move on to a writing project. This project will walk you through steps to plan, draft, revise, edit, and finally publish an essay or other piece of writing about one or more of the texts you have studied in the unit. Student models and graphic organizers will provide guidance and help you organize your thoughts as you plan and write your essay. Throughout the project, you will also study and work on specific writing skills to help you develop different portions of your writing.

UNIT 3   When should we stand up for others and ourselves?

Facing Challenges

 TEXTS

4	**A Wrinkle in Time** FICTION *Madeleine L'Engle*
10	**The Monsters Are Due on Maple Street** DRAMA *Rod Serling*
17	**Red Scarf Girl** NON-FICTION *Ji-Li Jiang*
22	**I Am an American: A True Story of Japanese Internment** NON-FICTION *Jerry Stanley*
27	**Roll of Thunder, Hear My Cry** FICTION *Mildred D. Taylor*
33	**Children of the Dust Bowl: The True Story of the School at Weedpatch Camp** NON-FICTION *Jerry Stanley*
38	**The Circuit: Stories From the Life of a Migrant Child** FICTION *Francisco Jimenez*
46	**Les Misérables** FICTION *Victor Hugo*

Please note that excerpts and passages in the StudySync® library and this workbook are intended as touchstones to generate interest in an author's work. The excerpts and passages do not substitute for the reading of entire texts, and StudySync® strongly recommends that students seek out and purchase the whole literary or informational work in order to experience it as the author intended. Links to online resellers are available in our digital library. In addition, complete works may be ordered through an authorized reseller by filling out and returning to StudySync® the order form enclosed in this workbook.

TEXTS

54 Jabberwocky
POETRY *Lewis Carroll*

58 Bullying in Schools
NON-FICTION *Point/Counterpoint*

EXTENDED WRITING PROJECT

66 Extended Writing Project: Narrative Writing

72 Extended Writing Project: Prewrite

74 **SKILL:** Organize Narrative Writing

79 **SKILL:** Descriptive Details

83 Extended Writing Project: Plan

86 **SKILL:** Introductions/Story Beginning

89 **SKILL:** Narrative Techniques and Sequencing

93 **SKILL:** Conclusions

96 Extended Writing Project: Draft

98 Extended Writing Project: Revise

101 Extended Writing Project: Edit, Proofread, and Publish

105

Text Fulfillment through StudySync

A WRINKLE IN TIME

FICTION
Madeleine L'Engle
1962

INTRODUCTION

Meg Murry and her precocious younger brother Charles will do anything they can to find their father. Did their father's top-secret experiments with time-travel cause his mysterious disappearance? What evil forces are holding him hostage? The children embark on a dangerous journey to find the answers, joined by their young neighbor, Calvin. In the excerpt below, they have arrived on Camazotz, a distant planet controlled by a sinister force. There they encounter a strange man with a fixed, red-eyed gaze. Telepathically, he urges them to merge their thoughts with his.

"Look into my eyes. Look deep within them and I will tell you."

FIRST READ

Excerpt from Chapter 7: The Man with Red Eyes

1. "Once ten is ten. Once eleven is eleven. Once twelve is twelve."

2. The number words pounded insistently against Meg's brain. They seemed to be **boring** their way into her skull.

3. "Twice one is two. Twice two is four. Twice three is six."

4. Calvin's voice came out in an angry shout. "Fourscore and seven years ago our fathers brought forth on this continent a new nation, conceived in liberty, and dedicated to the proposition that all men are created equal."

5. "Twice four is eight. Twice five is ten. Twice six is twelve."

6. "Father!" Meg screamed. "Father!" The scream, half involuntary, jerked her mind back out of darkness.

7. The words of the multiplication table seemed to break up into laughter. "Splendid! Splendid! You have passed your **preliminary** tests with flying colors."

8. "You didn't think we were as easy as all that, falling for that old stuff, did you?" Charles Wallace demanded.

9. "Ah, I hoped not. I most sincerely hoped not. But after all you are very young and very **impressionable,** and the younger the better, my little man. The younger the better."

10 Meg looked up at the fiery eyes, at the light pulsing above them, and then away. She tried looking at the mouth, at the thin, almost colorless lips, and this was more possible, even though she had to look **obliquely,** so that she was not sure exactly what the face really looked like, whether it was young or old, cruel or kind, human or alien.

11 "If you please," she said, trying to sound calm and brave. "The only reason we are here is because we think our father is here. Can you tell us where to find him?"

12 "Ah, your father!" There seemed to be a great chortling of delight. "Ah, yes, your father! It is not *can* I, you know, young lady, but *will* I?"

13 "Will you, then?"

14 "That depends on a number of things. Why do you want your father?"

15 "Didn't you ever have a father yourself?" Meg demanded. "You don't want him for a *reason*. You want him because he's your *father*."

16 "Ah, but he hasn't been *acting* very like a father, lately, has he? Abandoning his wife and his four little children to go **gallivanting** off on wild adventures of his own."

17 "He was working for the government. He'd never have left us otherwise. And we want to see him, please. Right now."

18 "My, but the little miss is impatient! Patience, patience, young lady."

19 Meg did not tell the man on the chair that patience was not one of her virtues.

20 "And by the way, my children," he continued blandly, "you don't need to vocalize verbally with me, you know. I can understand you quite as well as you can understand me."

21 Charles Wallace put his hands on his hips defiantly. "The spoken word is one of the triumphs of man," he proclaimed, "and I intend to continue using it, particularly with people I don't trust." But his voice was shaking. Charles Wallace, who even as an infant had seldom cried, was near tears.

22 "And you don't trust me?"

23 "What reason have you given us to trust you?"

24 "What cause have I given you for distrust?" The thin lips curled slightly.

25 Suddenly Charles Wallace darted forward and hit the man as hard as he could, which was fairly hard, as he had had a good deal of coaching from the twins.

26 "Charles!" Meg screamed.

27 The men in dark smocks moved smoothly but with swiftness to Charles. The man in the chair casually raised one finger, and the men dropped back.

28 "Hold it—" Calvin whispered, and together he and Meg darted forward and grabbed Charles Wallace, pulling him back from the platform.

29 The man gave a wince and the thought of his voice was a little breathless, as though Charles Wallace's punch had succeeded in winding him. "May I ask why you did that?"

30 "Because you aren't you," Charles Wallace said. "I'm not sure what you are, but you"—he pointed to the man on the chair—"aren't what's talking to us. I'm sorry if I hurt you. I didn't think you were real. I thought perhaps you were a robot, because I don't feel anything coming directly from you. I'm not sure where it's coming from, but it's coming through you. It isn't you."

31 "Pretty smart, aren't you?" the thought asked, and Meg had an uncomfortable feeling that she detected a snarl.

32 "It's not that I'm smart," Charles Wallace said, and again Meg could feel the palm of his hand sweating inside hers.

33 "Try to find out who I am, then," the thought probed.

34 "I have been trying," Charles Wallace said, his voice high and troubled.

35 "Look into my eyes. Look deep within them and I will tell you."

36 Charles Wallace looked quickly at Meg and Calvin, then said, as though to himself, "I have to," and focused his clear blue eyes on the red ones of the man in the chair. Meg looked not at the man but at her brother. After a moment it seemed that his eyes were no longer focusing. The pupils grew smaller and smaller, as though he were looking into an intensely bright light, until they seemed to close entirely, until his eyes were nothing but an opaque blue. He slipped his hands out of Meg's and Calvin's and started walking slowly toward the man on the chair.

37 "No!" Meg screamed. "No!"

38 But Charles Wallace continued his slow walk forward, and she knew that he had not heard her.

STUDYSYNC LIBRARY | A Wrinkle in Time

39 "No!" she screamed again, and ran after him. With her inefficient flying tackle she landed on him. She was so much larger than he that he fell sprawling, hitting his head a sharp crack against the marble floor. She knelt by him, sobbing. After a moment of lying there as though he had been knocked out by the blow, he opened his eyes, shook his head, and sat up. Slowly the pupils of his eyes dilated until they were back to normal, and the blood came back to his white cheeks.

40 The man on the chair spoke directly into Meg's mind, and now there was a distinct menace to the words. "I am not pleased," he said to her. "I could very easily lose patience with you, and that, for your information, young lady, would not be good for your father. If you have the slightest desire to see your father again, you had better cooperate."

Excerpted from *A Wrinkle in Time* by Madeleine L'Engle, published by Farrar, Strauss and Giroux.

THINK QUESTIONS

1. Explain how Meg, Calvin, and Charles Wallace communicate with the man with red eyes. Support your answer with textual evidence, referring both to ideas you infer from specific details and to information that is directly stated.

2. Use details from the text to write three or four sentences describing Charles Wallace.

3. Write three or four sentences explaining how the man with red eyes is able to manipulate the children. Support your answer with textual evidence.

4. Use context to determine the meaning of the word **boring** as it is used in *A Wrinkle in Time*. Write your definition of "boring" and explain how you got it. What else can "boring" mean, and how can you tell which meaning applies here?

5. Use context clues to determine the meaning of **impressionable** as it is used in *A Wrinkle in Time*. Write your definition of "impressionable" and tell how you determined it

CLOSE READ

Reread the excerpt from *A Wrinkle in Time*. As you reread, complete the Focus Questions below. Then use your answers and annotations from the questions to help you complete the Writing Prompt.

FOCUS QUESTIONS

1. Reread paragraphs 1–7, in which the red-eyed man tries to control Meg, Charles Wallace, and Calvin by infiltrating their thoughts with the multiplication table, something that is memorized and repeated without thought. Explain how Calvin and Meg each fend off the red-eyed man's mind-control advances. How do the children's responses differ? How do their differing responses contribute to what happens next in the plot? Highlight evidence from the text and make annotations to support your answers.

2. In paragraph 8, Charles Wallace demands, "You didn't think we were as easy as all that, falling for that old stuff, did you?" How does the red-eyed man respond to the question, and what can you infer about him from his response? Highlight evidence from the text and make annotations to explain your inferences.

3. In paragraphs 11–19, what strategy does Meg use to try to find out the whereabouts of her father? How effective are her efforts? What impact does her interaction with the red-eyed man have on the developing plot? Highlight textual evidence and make annotations to explain your ideas.

4. Why does Charles Wallace strike the red-eyed man, and how does the blow relate to the man's challenge to "find out who I am, then" in paragraph 33? Highlight and annotate textual evidence to demonstrate the effect Charles Wallace's actions have on plot development.

5. In paragraphs 37–39, how does Meg stand up for Charles Wallace? How does the relationship between the children and the red-eyed man begin to change at this point in the plot? Highlight and annotate textual evidence to support your answers.

WRITING PROMPT

In this excerpt from *A Wrinkle in Time*, the red-eyed man tries to control the minds of Meg, Charles Wallace, and Calvin. In what ways do the children stand up for themselves? How do their responses contribute to the unfolding plot? Explain how the children's determination and courage shape what happens in their confrontation with the mysterious red-eyed man. Maintain a formal style in your explanation, and use clear, precise language to help your readers understand this event in the story. Cite textual evidence to support your ideas.

THE MONSTERS ARE DUE ON MAPLE STREET

DRAMA
Rod Serling
1960

INTRODUCTION

Rod Serling, creator of the science fiction television series *The Twilight Zone*, was one of the most popular writers in television history. One of his best-known scripts, "The Monsters Are Due on Maple Street" is about the reaction of a group of neighbors to a mysterious shadow that passes over their suburban street. After homes lose power and car batteries go dead, a neighborhood boy suggests that alien invaders in human form are responsible for the strange events. As power flickers back on here and there, neighbors become increasingly alarmed, turning their suspicions against one another.

"Who do I talk to? I talk to monsters from outer space."

 FIRST READ

1. *From Act I*

2. GOODMAN. Wait a minute now. You keep your distance—all of you. So I've got a car that starts by itself—well, that's a freak thing, I admit it. But does that make me some kind of a criminal or something? I don't know why the car works—it just does!

3. [*This stops the crowd momentarily and now* GOODMAN, *still backing away, goes toward the front porch. He goes up the steps and then stops to stand facing the mob.*

4. *We see a long shot of* STEVE *as he comes through the crowd.*]

5. STEVE. [*Quietly.*] We're all on a monster kick, Les. Seems that the general impression holds that maybe one family isn't what we think they are. Monsters from outer space or something. Different than us. Fifth columnists from the vast beyond. [*He chuckles.*] You know anybody that might fit that description around here on Maple Street?

6. GOODMAN. What is this, a gag or something? This a practical joke or something?

7. [*We see a close-up of the porch light as it suddenly goes out. There's a murmur from the group.*]

8. GOODMAN. Now I suppose that's supposed to **incriminate** me! The light goes on and off. That really does it, doesn't it? [*He look around the faces of the people.*] I just don't understand this—[*He wets his lips, looking from face to face.*] Look, you all know me. We've lived here five years. Right in this house. We're no different from any of the rest of you! We're no different at all. Really . . . this whole thing is just . . . just weird—

9 WOMAN. Well, if that's the case, Les Goodman, explain why—[*She stops suddenly, clamping her mouth shut.*]

10 GOODMAN. [*Softly.*] Explain what?

11 STEVE. [*Interjecting*] Look, let's forget this—

12 CHARLIE. [*Overlapping him.*] Go ahead, let her talk. What about it? Explain what?

13 WOMAN. [*A little reluctantly.*] Well . . . sometimes I go to bed late at night. A couple of times... a couple of times I'd come out on the porch and I'd see Mr. Goodman here in the wee hours of the morning standing out in front of his house . . . looking up at the sky. [*She looks around the circle of faces.*] That's right, looking up at the sky as if . . . as if he were waiting for something. [*A pause.*] As if he were looking for something.

14 [*There's a murmur of reaction from the crowd again.*

15 *We cut suddenly to a group shot.* As GOODMAN *starts toward them, they back away frightened.*]

16 GOODMAN. You know really . . . this is for laughs. You know what I'm guilty of? [*He laughs.*] I'm guilty of **insomnia....**

17 *From Act II*

18 CHARLIE'S VOICE. [*Shrill, from across the street.*] You best watch who you're seen with, Steve! Until we get this all straightened out, you ain't exactly above suspicion yourself.

19 STEVE. [*Whirling around toward him.*] Or you, Charlie. Or any of us, it seems. From age eight on up.

20 WOMAN. What I'd like to know is—what are we gonna do? Just stand around here all night?

21 CHARLIE. There's nothin' else we can do! [*He turns back looking toward* STEVE *and* GOODMAN *again.*] One of 'em'll tip their hand. They got to.

22 STEVE [*Raising his voice.*] There's something you can do, Charlie. You could go home and keep your mouth shut. You could quit strutting around like a self-appointed hanging judge and just climb into bed and forget it.

23 CHARLIE. You sound real anxious to have that happen, Steve. I think we better keep our eye on you too!

24   DON. [*As if he were taking the bit in his teeth, takes a hesitant step to the front.*] I think everything might as well come out now. [*He turns toward* STEVE.] Your wife's done plenty of talking, Steve, about how odd you are!

25   CHARLIE. [*Picking this up, his eyes widening.*] Go ahead, tell us what she's said. [*We see a long shot of* STEVE *as he walks toward them from across the street.*]

26   STEVE. Go ahead, what's my wife said? Let's get it all out. Let's pick out every **idiosyncrasy** of every man, woman, and child on the street. And then we might as well set up some kind of kangaroo court. How about a firing squad at dawn, Charlie, so we can get rid of all the suspects? Narrow them down. Make it easier for you.

27   DON. There's no need gettin' so upset, Steve. It's just that . . . well . . . Myra's talked about how there's been plenty of nights you spent hours down in your basement workin' on some kind of radio or something. Well, none of us have ever seen that radio—

28   [*By this time* STEVE *has reached the group. He stands there defiantly close to them.*]

29   CHARLIE. Go ahead, Steve. What kind of "radio set" you workin' on? I never seen it. Neither has anyone else. Who you talk to on that radio set? And who talks to you?

30   STEVE. I'm surprised at you, Charlie. How come you're so **dense** all of a sudden? [*A pause.*] Who do I talk to? I talk to monsters from outer space. I talk to three-headed green men who fly over here in what look like meteors.

31   [STEVE'S *wife steps down from the porch, bites her lip, calls out.*]

32   MRS. BRAND. Steve! Steve, please. [*Then looking around, frightened, she walks toward the group.*] It's just a ham radio set, that's all. I bought him a book on it myself. It's just a ham radio set. A lot of people have them. I can show it to you. It's right down in the basement.

33   STEVE. [*whirls around toward her*]Show them nothing! If they want to look inside our house—let them get a search warrant.

34   CHARLIE. Look, buddy. You can't afford to—

35   STEVE. [*Interrupting*]Charlie, don't tell me what I can afford! And stop telling me who's dangerous and who isn't and who's safe and who's a menace. [*He turns to the group and shouts.*]And you're with him, too—all of you! You're standing here all set to crucify—all set to find a scapegoat—all desperate to

point some kind of finger at a neighbor! Well now look, friends, the only thing that's gonna happen is that we'll eat each other up alive—

36   [*He stops abruptly as CHARLIE suddenly grabs his arm.*]

37   CHARLIE. [*In a hushed voice*]That's not the only thing that can happen to us.

38   [*Cut to a long shot looking down the street. A figure has suddenly materialized in the gloom and in the silence we can hear the clickety-clack of slow, measured footsteps on concrete as the figure walks slowly toward them. One of the women lets out a stifled cry. The young mother grabs her boy as do a couple of others.*]

39   TOMMY. [*Shouting, frightened.*] It's the monster! It's the monster!

40   [*Another woman lets out a wail and the people fall back in a group, staring toward the darkness and the approaching figure.*

41   *We see a medium group shot of the people as they stand in the shadows watching.* DON MARTIN *joins them, carrying a shotgun. He holds it up.*]

42   DON. We may need this.

43   STEVE. A shotgun? [*He pulls it out of* DON'S *hand.*] Good Lord—will anybody think a thought around here? Will you people wise up? What good would a shotgun do against—

44   [*Now CHARLIE pulls the gun from STEVE's hand.*]

45   CHARLIE. No more talk, Steve. You're going to talk us into a grave! You'd let whatever's out there walk right over us, wouldn't yuh? Well, some of us won't!

46   [*He swings the gun around to point it toward the sidewalk. The dark figure continues to walk toward them.*

47   *The group stands there, fearful, apprehensive, mother's clutching children, men standing in front of wives. CHARLIE slowly raises the gun. As the figure gets closer and closer he suddenly pulls the trigger. The sound of it explodes in the stillness. There is a long angle shot looking down the figure, who suddenly lets out a small cry, stumbles forward onto his knees and then falls forward on his face. DON, CHARLIE, and STEVE race forward over to him. STEVE is there first and turns the man over. Now the crowd gathers around them.*]

48   STEVE [*Slowly looks up*] It's Pete Van Horn.

49 DON. [*In a hushed voice.*] Pete Van Horn! He was just gonna go over to the next block to see if the power was on—

50 WOMAN. You killed him, Charlie. You shot him dead!

51 CHARLIE. [*Looks around the circle of faces, his eyes frightened, his face **contorted**.*] But . . . but I didn't know who he was. I certainly didn't know who he was. He comes walkin' out of the darkness—how am I supposed to know who he was? [*He grabs* STEVE.] Steve—you know why I shot! How was I supposed to know he wasn't a monster or something? [*He grabs* DON *now.*] We're all scared of the same thing, I was just tryin' to . . . trying' to protect my home, that's all! Look, all of you, that's all I was tryin' to do. [*He looks down wildly at the body.*] I didn't know it was somebody we knew! I didn't know—

52 [*There's a sudden hush and then an intake of breath. We see a medium shot of the living room window of* CHARLIE'S *house. The window is not lit, but suddenly the house lights come on behind it.*]

53 WOMAN. [*In a very hushed voice.*] Charlie. . . Charlie. . . the lights just went on in your house. Why did the lights just go on?

54 DON. What about it, Charlie? How come you're the only one with lights now?

55 GOODMAN. That's what I'd like to know.

© 1960 by Rod Serling, *The Monsters Are Due on Maple Street.* Reproduced by permission of Carolyn Serling.

THINK QUESTIONS

1. Refer to details from the text to explain why the Maple Street neighbors are suspicious of Les Goodman. Include both ideas that are directly stated and ideas that you have inferred from clues in the text.

2. Use details from the text to write two or three sentences explaining why the Maple Street neighbors are suspicious of Steve.

3. Write two or three sentences explaining why Tommy shouts, "It's the monster! It's the monster!" Support your answer with textual evidence.

4. The Latin root *tort* or *torq* means "to twist or turn." The Latin affix *con-* means "together." Use these meanings, along with context clues in the text, to determine the meaning of **contorted** as it is used in "The Monsters Are Due On Maple Street." Write your definition of "contorted" and explain how you found it.

5. The Latin prefix *in-* means "in or into," and the Latin root *crim* means "crime." The suffix *–ate,* used with a verb, often means "cause to become." Use the Latin root and affix, along with context clues provided in the passage, to determine the meaning of **incriminate** as it is used in the text. Write your definition of "incriminate" and tell how you found it.

STUDYSYNC LIBRARY | The Monsters Are Due on Maple Street

CLOSE READ

Reread the excerpt from "The Monsters Are Due on Maple Street." As you reread, complete the Focus Questions below. Then use your answers and annotations from the questions to help you complete the Writing Prompt.

FOCUS QUESTIONS

1. How does the monster in *A Wrinkle in Time* compare and contrast with the monster in "The Monsters Are Due on Maple Street"? Support your response with textual evidence and make annotations to explain your ideas.

2. Based on Acts I and II, in what ways do Les Goodman and Charlie change roles as the plot moves toward resolution? Highlight textual evidence and make annotations to explain your response.

3. Based on Act II, how do Tommy's and Steve's responses to events contribute to the story's resolution? Highlight textual evidence and make annotations to support your explanation.

4. Compare the actions and reactions of the children in the novel *A Wrinkle in Time* with those of the adults in the teleplay "The Monsters Are Due on Maple Street," considering the way each deals with the element of fear. How do the characters' responses have an impact, either positively or negatively, on the situation they find themselves in? Highlight textual evidence and make annotations to support your explanation.

5. In "The Monsters Are Due on Maple Street," in what ways do the characters stand up for or fail to stand up for themselves? Highlight textual evidence and make annotations to explain your ideas.

WRITING PROMPT

In both *A Wrinkle in Time* and "The Monsters Are Due on Maple Street," the characters ask questions for a number of different reasons. Compare and contrast the questions asked by Meg and Charles Wallace with the questions asked by the red-eyed man in *A Wrinkle in Time* and by the neighbors in "The Monsters Are Due on Maple Street." What do these questions tell the reder about the theme of seeking the truth? How is this theme portrayed similarly and differently in the excerpts from the novel and the script? Support the claim or claims you make in your comparison and contrast with evidence from both texts.

RED SCARF GIRL:
A MEMOIR OF THE CULTURAL REVOLUTION

NON-FICTION
Ji-Li Jiang
1997

INTRODUCTION

Ji-Li Jiang grew up dedicated to the Communist Party, and was embarrassed by her family's "landlord" background during the Cultural Revolution. However, her feelings began to change when the government started attacking her family. In this excerpt, she has been pulled out of class and is being interrogated by people from her father's theater.

"We want you to testify against your father..."

FIRST READ

1 "Sit down, sit down. Don't be afraid." Chairman Jin pointed to the empty chair. "These comrades from your father's work unit are just here to have a study session with you. It's nothing to worry about."

2 I sat down dumbly.

3 I had thought about their coming to my home but never imagined this. They were going to expose my family in front of my teachers and classmates. I would have no pride left. I would never be an **educable** child again.

4 Thin-Face sat opposite me, with a woman I had never seen before. Teacher Zhang was there too, his eyes encouraging me.

5 Thin-Face came straight to the point. "Your father's problems are very serious. " His cold eyes nailed me to my seat. "You may have read the article in the *Workers' Revolt* that exposed your family's filthy past." I slumped down in my chair without taking my eyes off his face. "In addition to coming from a landlord family, your father committed some serious mistakes during the Antirightist Movement several years ago, but he still obstinately refuses to confess." His cold manner became a little more animated. "Of course we won't tolerate this. We have decided to make an example of him. We are going to have a struggle meeting of the entire theater system to criticize him and force him to confess." He suddenly pounded the table with his fist. The cups on the table rattled.

6 I tore my eyes away from him and stared at a cup instead.

7 "As I told you before, you are your own person. If you want to make a clean break with your black family, then you can be an educable child and we will

welcome you to our revolutionary ranks." He gave Chairman Jin a look, and Chairman Jin chimed in, "That's right, we welcome you."

8. "Jiang Ji-li has always done well at school. In addition to doing very well in her studies, she participates in educational **reform**," Teacher Zhang added.

9. "That's very good. We knew that you had more sense than to follow your father," Thin-Face said with a brief, frozen smile. "Now you can show your revolutionary determination." He paused. "We want you to **testify** against your father at the struggle meeting."

10. I closed my eyes. I saw Dad standing on a stage, his head bowed, his name written in large black letters, and then crossed out in red ink, on a sign hanging from his neck. I saw myself standing in the middle of the stage, facing thousands of people, **condemning** Dad for his crimes, raising my fist to lead the chant, "Down with Jiang Xi-reng." I saw Dad looking at me hopelessly, tears on his face.

11. "I...I..." I looked at Teacher Zhang for help. He looked away.

12. The Woman from the theater spoke. "It's really not such a hard thing to do. The key is your class stance. The daughter of our former Party Secretary resolved to make a clean break with her mother. When she went onstage to condemn her mother, she actually slapped her face. Of course, we don't mean that you have to slap your father's face. The point is that as long as you have the correct class stance, it will be easy to testify." Her voice grated on my ears.

13. "There is something you can do to prove you are truly Chairman Mao's child." Thin-Face spoke again. "I am sure you can tell us some things your father said and did that show his landlord and rightist mentality." I stared at the table, but I could feel his eyes boring into me. "What can you tell us?"

14. "But I don't know anything," I whispered." I don't know—"

15. "I am sure you can remember something if you think about it," Thin-Face said. "A man like him could not hide his true beliefs from a child as smart as you. He must have made comments critical of Chairman Mao and the Cultural Revolution. I am sure you are loyal to Chairman Mao and the Communist Party. Tell us!"

16. "But my father never said anything against Chairman Mao," I protested weakly. "I would tell you if he did." My voice grew stronger with **conviction**. "He never said anything against the Party."

STUDYSYNC LIBRARY | Red Scarf Girl

17 "Now, you have to choose between two roads." Thin-Face looked straight into my eyes. "You can break with your family and follow Chairman Mao, or you can follow your father and become an enemy of the people." His voice grew more severe. "In that case we would have many more study sessions, with your brother and sister too, and the Red Guard Committee and the school leaders. Think about it. We will come back to talk to you again."

18 Thin-Face and the woman left, saying they would be back to get my statement. Without knowing how I got there, I found myself in a narrow passageway between the school building and the school-yard wall. The gray concrete walls closed around me and a slow drizzle dampened my cheeks. I could not go back to the classroom, and I could not go home. I felt like a small animal that had fallen into a trap, alone and helpless, and sure that the hunter was coming.

Excerpted from *Red Scarf Girl* by Ji-li Jiang, published by HarperCollins Publishers.

THINK QUESTIONS

1. How does Ji-Li feel about being called to the study session? Cite textual evidence to support your answer.

2. What problem does Ji-Li's father face? Why? Cite evidence from the text in support of your answer.

3. What choice does Ji-Li face? What will be the consequences of her choice? Support your answer with textual evidence.

4. Use context to determine the meaning of the word **condemning** as it is used in *Red Scarf Girl*. Write your definition of "condemning" and tell how you arrived at it.

5. Remembering that the Latin suffix *-able* means "able to do or to have done" and that the Latin root *educare* means "to teach, to bring up," use the context clues provided in the passage to determine the meaning of **educable.** Write your definition of "educable" and tell how you arrived at it. Can you think of any words that are related to "educable"? How might they be related to it?

STUDYSYNC LIBRARY | **Red Scarf Girl**

CLOSE READ

Reread the excerpt from *Red Scarf Girl*. As you reread, complete the Focus Questions below. Then use your answers and annotations from the questions to help you complete the Writing Prompt.

FOCUS QUESTIONS

1. In paragraph 5, the narrator describes Thin-Face's "manner." Use context clues to determine the meaning of the word "animated," and explain what connotations "animated" has in this context. Highlight and make annotations to identify and explain any word relationships that helped you determine the word's meaning and connotations.

2. In paragraphs 9–13, as the Party officials continue talking to Ji-Li, what do they wish to achieve? How do they get their ideas across? Highlight evidence from the text and make annotations to support your answer.

3. In paragraphs 14–16, Ji-Li tells the Party officials that her father is innocent and that she doesn't know anything that would condemn him. Do key details in the text, including Ji-Li's own words, support her explanation? Why or why not? Highlight textual evidence and make annotations to support your answer.

4. In the final paragraph of the selection, Ji-Li describes the physical details of her surroundings. How do the connotations of the words she chooses contribute to your understanding of the events that have happened, and of Ji-Li's feelings about them? Highlight textual evidence and make annotations to explain your ideas.

5. The events of the study session force Ji-Li to face a new challenge. How will the decision she makes affect not only her own life but the lives of her family members as well? Highlight textual evidence and make annotations to support your answer.

WRITING PROMPT

Based on the events, facts, and details in the text, what arguments could be made for Ji-Li to condemn her father, and what arguments could be made for her to stand by him? Present at least two reasons for each side. Make sure that each reason is supported by evidence from the text. Quote at least one specific phrase, sentence, or passage from the text, and show how the connotations or denotations support a specific side of the argument. Try to make both sides of the argument as strong and convincing as possible, no matter which side you personally agree with. (You do not have to say which one you agree with.)

I AM AN AMERICAN:
A TRUE STORY OF JAPANESE INTERNMENT

NON-FICTION
Jerry Stanley
1996

INTRODUCTION

As described in author Jerry Stanley's non-fiction work *I Am an American*, Japanese Americans went to great lengths to show their loyalty to the United States after the Japanese attack on Pearl Harbor in 1941. However, despite initial political support for Japanese-Americans, military officials expressed concern that they might help Japan invade the West Coast. As a result of public fear and pressure, the U.S. government ordered the forced evacuation of more than 100,000 Japanese Americans from their homes to internment camps. The excerpt explores this period of war hysteria and racism in American history.

"We in our hearts know we are Americans, loyal to America."

FIRST READ

From Chapter 2: EXECUTIVE ORDER NO. 9066

1. After Pearl Harbor the Nisei went to great lengths to demonstrate their **patriotism.** They flooded the streets of San Francisco, Los Angeles, and Seattle in mass **demonstrations** of loyalty. They waved American flags and recited the pledge of the Japanese American Citizens League. They bought war bonds, donated blood, and ran ads in newspapers denouncing Japan and pledging loyalty to America. In San Francisco, Nisei started a fund-raising campaign to buy bombs for attacking Tokyo. In Los Angeles they formed committees to make sure that no person of Japanese ancestry tried to aid Japan. The day after Pearl Harbor the Japanese American Citizens League sent the following telegram to President Roosevelt:

2. In this solemn hour we pledge our fullest cooperation to you, Mr. President, and to our country. There can not be any question. . . . We in our hearts know we are Americans, loyal to America.

3. At first, the demonstrations of loyalty brought pledges of support from government officials, and Japanese **internmen**t seemed unlikely. California Congressman Leland Ford said, "These people are American-born. This is their country." United States Attorney General Francis Biddle declared, "At no time will the government engage in wholesale **condemnation** of any alien group."

4. The only action Biddle took in December was to move against enemy aliens—that is, German, Italian, and Japanese citizens living in the United States. He ordered the Federal Bureau of Investigation to arrest approximately 16,000 enemy aliens suspected of espionage or **sabotage,** but within weeks he released two-thirds of them. At the same time, the FBI and the Federal Communications Commission conducted separate investigations of the

Japanese living in America. Both investigations concluded that the Nisei were loyal citizens and that their Issei parents had taken no action to aid Japan.

5   It was a series of Japanese victories in the Pacific that started the movement to intern the Japanese. Japan captured Guam on December 13, 1941, Hong Kong on December 24, Manila on January 2, 1942, and Singapore on February 15.

6   Alarmed at the enemy's swift advance through the Pacific, military officials suggested that Japan might try to invade the west coast of America and that maybe the Issei and the Nisei who lived there would aid the invasion. The Western Defense Commander, Lieutenant General John L. DeWitt, who was responsible for the security of the Pacific coast, was influential in spreading the idea that the Japanese might be disloyal. Following the loss of Manila he said, "I have little confidence that the Japanese enemy aliens [Issei] are loyal. I have no confidence in the loyalty of the Nisei whatsoever."

7   DeWitt's distrust appeared to be confirmed in the Roberts Report, a government investigation of the bombing of Pearl Harbor. Issued at about the time Singapore fell to Japan in February, the report blamed the disaster on lack of military preparedness and on Japanese sabotage in Hawaii. It even suggested that Japanese farmers had planted their crops in the shape of arrows pointing to Pearl Harbor as the target.

8   Although the charge of Japanese sabotage on Hawaii was totally false, newspaper writers and radio broadcasters began warning of the danger of Japanese sabotage on the west coast. In Los Angeles, radio commentator John Hughes warned that "Ninety percent or more of American-born Japanese are primarily loyal to Japan."

...

9   Stunned by the growing hostility, the Nisei tried to appear as un-Japanese as possible. Slowly, sadly, all along the west coast of America, they destroyed what they possessed of their Asian heritage. Japanese books and magazines were burned because of a rumor that FBI agents had found such materials in the homes of Issei arrested on suspicion of sabotage. Priceless diaries, letters, and photographs were burned; porcelain vases, tea sets, and silk tablecloths were buried or dumped on the street.

...

10 By mid-February the entire coastline of California was designated Restricted Area Number One. DeWitt issued a stern suggestion that the Japanese living in this coastal strip should voluntarily migrate inland. But when some 4,000

tried to move, they were met with hostility. Armed men patrolled the Nevada border to turn them back while main streets in Utah sported signs reading "No Japs Wanted." Because most people in the inland states had never met a person of Japanese ancestry, they decided that if the Japanese were a threat to California then they were also a threat to them.

. . .

11. With no personal knowledge of the Japanese living in America, President Franklin D. Roosevelt yielded to pressure from the California Hotheads, the media, and the military. On February 19, 1942, Roosevelt signed Executive Order No. 9066, which gave the military the authority to remove enemy aliens and anyone else suspected of disloyalty. Although the document never mentioned the Japanese by name, it was understood that the order was meant for them alone.

"Executive Order No. 9066 (Chapter 2)" from I AM AN AMERICAN: A TRUE STORY OF JAPANESE INTERNMENT by Jerry Stanley, copyright © 1994 by Jerry Stanley. Used by permission of Crown Publishers, an imprint of Random House Children's Books, a division of Random House LLC. All rights reserved.

THINK QUESTIONS

1. Explain how and why the Nisei went to great lengths to demonstrate patriotism after the bombing of Pearl Harbor. In your response, refer to details from the text to support ideas that are directly stated and ideas that you have inferred.

2. Use details from the text to write two or three sentences explaining how U.S. Attorney Francis Biddle's public statement regarding aliens contradicted his actions.

3. Write two or three sentences explaining the reasons given for Japanese internment. Support your answer with textual evidence.

4. Use context to determine the meaning of the word **demonstrations** as it is used in the first sentence of *I Am an American: A True Story of Japanese Internment*. Write your definition of "demonstrations" here and tell how you got it. Then, use a dictionary to verify your definition.

5. Remembering that the suffix *-ism* often means "a belief in" or "a state of action" and the Latin root *pater* means "father," use the context clues provided in the passage to determine the meaning of **patriotism.** Write your definition of "patriotism" and tell how you arrived at it. Use a dictionary to verify your answer.

STUDYSYNC LIBRARY | I Am an American: A True Story of Japanese Internment

CLOSE READ

Reread the excerpt from *I Am an American: A True Story of Japanese Internment*. As you reread, complete the Focus Questions below. Then use your answers and annotations from the questions to help you complete the Writing Prompt.

FOCUS QUESTIONS

1. In paragraphs 1 and 2, Stanley describes the reaction of Japanese Americans to the bombing of Pearl Harbor. How and why did Japanese Americans stand up for themselves? Highlight evidence in the text to support your ideas, and make annotations to explain your response.

2. As you reread the text of *I Am an American: A True Story of Japanese Internment*, consider the author's possible purposes for writing: to inform, to persuade, to describe, to explain, or to entertain. Remember that an author may write for more than one purpose. Based on paragraphs 3, 4, and 5, describe two possible purposes Stanley might have for writing. Highlight textual evidence that supports your response, and make annotations to explain your thinking.

3. In paragraphs 7 and 8, Stanley discusses the Roberts Report, a government investigation of the bombing of Pearl Harbor. What is Stanley's point of view regarding this report? Highlight evidence in the text to support your ideas, and make annotations to explain your thinking.

4. In paragraph 9, the author describes the destruction of cultural artifacts by Japanese Americans. Highlight textual evidence that indicates Stanley's point of view about this development, and annotate ideas that explain how he conveys it.

5. What clues in the text tell you how and why the U.S. government changed its mind about the American-born Nisei? How did this change of mind unfold? Highlight textual evidence and make annotations to explain your response.

WRITING PROMPT

Compare and contrast the points of view of the author, the government officials mentioned in the excerpt, and the Nisei themselves. How do these points of view compare? How does each party approach the question of how to deal with conflict—when to stand up and when to stand down? Support your writing with evidence from the text.

ROLL OF THUNDER, HEAR MY CRY

FICTION
Mildred D. Taylor
1976

INTRODUCTION

Mildred D. Taylor's gripping novel tells the story of the Logans, a land-owning black family in the Deep South struggling to keep things together during a tumultuous year in the 1930's. Largely insulated from the injustices of the world around her, but raised with a strong sense of fairness, nine-year old Cassie is only beginning to realize the realities of racism, including the everyday source of fear it presents to adults in her community. In the excerpt here, neighbors bring bad news for her father.

"...he's not gonna let a few smart colored folks ruin his business."

FIRST READ

From Chapter 9

1. When supper was ready, I eagerly grabbed the iron bell before Christopher-John or Little Man could claim it, and ran onto the back porch to summon Papa, Mr. Morrison, and Stacey from the fields. As the three of them washed up on the back porch, Mama went to the end of the porch where Papa stood alone. "What did Mr. Jamison want?" she asked, her voice barely **audible.**

2. Papa took the towel Mama handed him, but did not reply immediately. I was just inside the kitchen dipping out the butter beans. I moved closer to the window so that I could hear his answer.

3. "Don't keep anything from me, David. If there's trouble, I want to know."

4. Papa looked down at her. "Nothing to worry 'bout, honey . . . . just seems that Thurston Wallace been in town talking 'bout how he's not gonna let a few smart colored folks ruin his business. Says he's gonna put a stop to this shopping in Vicksburg. That's all."

5. Mama sighed and stared out across the plowed field to the sloping pasture land. "I'm feeling scared, David," she said.

6. Papa put down the towel. "Not yet, Mary. It's not time to be scared yet. They're just talking."

7. Mama turned and faced him. "And when they stop talking?"

8. "Then . . . then maybe it'll be time. But right now, pretty lady," he said, leading her by the hand toward the kitchen door, "right now I've got better things to think about."

9. Quickly I poured the rest of the butter beans into the bowl and hurried across the kitchen to the table. As Mama and Papa entered, I slid onto the bench beside Little Man and Christopher-John. Papa beamed down at the table.

10. "Well, look-a-here!" he exclaimed. "Good ole butter beans and cornbread! You better come on, Mr. Morrison! You too, son!" he called. "These womenfolks done gone and fixed us a feast."

11. After school was out, spring drooped quickly toward summer; yet Papa had not left for the railroad. He seemed to be waiting for something, and I secretly hoped that whatever that something was, it would never come so that he would not leave. But one evening as he, Mama, Big Ma, Mr. Morrison, and Stacey sat on the front porch while Christopher-John, Little Man, and I dashed around the yard chasing fireflies, I overheard him say, "Sunday I'm gonna have to go. Don't want to though. I got this gut feeling it ain't over yet. It's too easy."

12. I released the firefly **imprisoned** in my hand and sat beside Papa and Stacey on the steps. "Papa, please," I said, leaning against his leg, "don't go this year." Stacey looked out into the falling night, his face resigned, and said nothing.

13. Papa put out his large hand and caressed my face. "Got to, Cassie girl," he said softly. "Baby, there's bills to pay and ain't no money coming in. Your mama's got no job come fall and there's the **mortgage** and next year's taxes to think of."

14. "But, Papa, we planted more cotton this year. Won't that pay the taxes?"

15. Papa shook his head. "With Mr. Morrison here we was able to plant more, but that cotton is for living on; the railroad money is for the taxes and the mortgage."

16. I looked back at Mama wanting her to speak, to persuade him to stay, but when I saw her face I knew that she would not. She had known he would leave, just as we all had known.

17. "Papa, just another week or two, couldn't you—"

18. "I can't, baby. May have lost my job already."

19. "But Papa—"

20. "Cassie, that's enough now," Mama said from the deepening shadows.

21. I grew quiet and Papa put his arms around Stacey and me, his hands falling casually over our shoulders. From the edge of the lawn where Little Man and

Christopher-John had ventured after lightning bugs, Little Man called, "Somebody's coming!" A few minutes later Mr. Avery and Mr. Lanier emerged from the dusk and walked up the sloping lawn. Mama sent Stacey and me to get more chairs for the porch, then we settled back beside Papa still sitting on the steps, his back propped against a pillar facing the visitors.

22 "You goin' up to the store tomorrow, David?" Mr. Avery asked after all the amenities had been said. Since the first trip in January, Mr. Morrison had made one other trip to Vicksburg, but Papa had not gone with him.

23 Papa motioned to Mr. Morrison. "Mr. Morrison and me going the day after tomorrow. Your wife brought down that list of things you need yesterday."

24 Mr. Avery cleared his throat nervously. "It's—it's that list I come 'bout, David. . . . I don't want them things no more."

25 The porch grew silent.

26 When no one said anything, Mr. Avery glanced at Mr. Lanier, and Mr. Lanier shook his head and continued. "Mr. Granger making it hard on us, David. Said we gonna have to give him sixty percent of the cotton, 'stead of fifty . . . now that the cotton's planted and it's too late to plant more. . . . Don't s'pose though that it makes much difference. The way cotton sells these days, seems the more we plant, the less money we gets anyways—"

27 Mr. Avery's coughing interrupted him and he waited patiently until the coughing had stopped before he went on. "I'm gonna be hard put to pay that debt in Vicksburg, David, but I'm gonna. . . . I want you to know that."

. . .

28 Mr. Avery's coughing started again and for a while there was only the coughing and the silence. But when the coughing ceased, Mr. Lanier said, "I pray to God there was a way we could stay in this thing, but we can't go on no chain gang, David."

29 Papa nodded. "Don't expect you to, Silas."

30 Mr. Avery laughed softly. "We sure had 'em goin' for a time though, didn't we?"

31 "Yes," agreed Papa quietly, "we sure did."

32 When the men had left, Stacey snapped, "They got no right pulling out! Just 'cause them Wallaces threaten them one time they go jumping all over themselves to get out like a bunch of scared jackrabbits—"

33 Papa stood suddenly and grabbed Stacey upward. "You, boy, don't you get so grown you go to talking 'bout more than you know. Them men, they doing

what they've gotta do. You got any idea what a risk they took just to go shopping in Vicksburg in the first place? They go on that chain gang and their families got nothing. They'll get kicked off that plot of land they tend and there'll be no place for them to go. You understand that?"

34. "Y-yessir," said Stacey. Papa released him and stared moodily into the night. "You were born blessed, boy, with land of your own. If you hadn't been, you'd cry out for it while you try to survive . . . like Mr. Lanier and Mr. Avery. Maybe even do what they doing now. It's hard on a man to give up, but sometimes it seems there just ain't nothing else he can do."

35. "I . . . I'm sorry, Papa," Stacey muttered.

36. After a moment, Papa reached out and draped his arm over Stacey's shoulder.

37. "Papa," I said, standing to join them, "we giving up too?"

38. Papa looked down at me and brought me closer, then waved his hand toward the drive. "You see that fig tree over yonder, Cassie? Them other trees all around . . . that oak and walnut, they're a lot bigger and they take up more room and give so much shade they almost **overshadow** that little ole fig. But that fig tree's got roots that run deep, and it belongs in that yard as much as that oak and walnut. It keeps on blooming, bearing good fruit year after year, knowing all the time it'll never get as big as them other trees. Just keeps on growing and doing what it gotta do. It don't give up. It give up, it'll die. There's a lesson to be learned from that little tree, Cassie girl, 'cause we're like it. We keep doing what we gotta, and we don't give up. We can't."

Excerpted from *Roll of Thunder, Hear My Cry* by Mildred D. Taylor, published by Puffin Books.

THINK QUESTIONS

1. What major problems do Papa and the other characters face in this excerpt? Cite textual evidence to support your answer.

2. Why don't Mr. Avery and Mr. Lanier join in Papa's plan to try to solve the problem? Support your answer with evidence from the text.

3. In what way is the Logan family in a better economic position than their neighbors? How could that fact affect the Logans' willingness to stand up for themselves against racism? Cite textual evidence to support your answer.

4. Use context to determine the meaning of the word ventured as it is used in *Roll of Thunder, Hear My Cry*. Write your definition of "ventured" and tell how you got it.

5. The prefix *aud-* comes from the Latin word meaning "to hear," and the suffix *-ible* means "able to be." Use the word parts and the context clues in the passage to determine the meaning of audible. Write your definition of **"audible"** and tell how you got it.

STUDYSYNC LIBRARY | *Roll of Thunder, Hear My Cry*

CLOSE READ

Reread the excerpt from *Roll of Thunder, Hear My Cry*. As you reread, complete the Focus Questions below. Then use your answers and annotations from the questions to help you complete the Writing Prompt.

FOCUS QUESTIONS

1. What information do readers learn in the first two paragraphs of *Roll of Thunder, Hear My Cry*? Highlight evidence from the text and make annotations noting specific reasons for your answer.

2. In paragraphs 3–8, what does the dialogue between Mama and Papa reveal about the problem they face and the way they each deal with it? How does this contribute to the development of the story's plot? Highlight specific evidence from the text and make annotations to support your answer.

3. In paragraphs 11–17, what key words and phrases does the author use to indicate the passage of time and move the plot forward? What inference can readers make about why Papa has delayed leaving the farm? Highlight specific words, phrases, or sentences from the text and make annotations to explain your answer.

4. In paragraphs 22–26, how does the conversation Papa has with Mr. Avery and Mr. Lanier relate to his earlier conversation with Mama? How is the language used in this conversation different from his earlier discussion, and what does it suggest about the characters? Highlight textual evidence and make annotations to explain your ideas.

5. In paragraphs 33–38, Papa talks with Stacey, and then with Cassie. In these passages, what do Stacey and Cassie learn from Papa about the importance of standing up for themselves and for others? What theme, or message, do Papa's words express? Highlight evidence from the text and make annotations to explain your ideas.

WRITING PROMPT

Analyze how the story structure Mildred Taylor chose to use in this chapter of her novel *Roll of Thunder, Hear My Cry* helped you to understand and appreciate the text. In your analysis, be sure to include examples of particular events and characterization, including the language and dialect various characters use. Examine and explain how the examples fit into the overall structure of the text. How did they help to develop the story's plot and message? Cite evidence from the text to support your ideas.

CHILDREN OF THE DUSTBOWL

THE TRUE STORY OF THE SCHOOL AT WEEDPATCH CAMP

NON-FICTION
Jerry Stanley
1993

INTRODUCTION

In the 1930s, drought and dust storms severely damaged the prairies of the United States, resulting in a period known as the Dust Bowl. Tens of thousands of families abandoned their destroyed farms in the Midwest and migrated to California and other states looking for work, but because of the Great Depression, many were unsuccessful. *Children of the Dust Bowl: The True Story of the School at Weedpatch Camp* is a nonfiction book about the period that focuses on educator Leo Hart and his role in creating a "federal emergency school" for the children of Weedpatch Camp, one of the farm-labor camps built by the federal government to house migrant workers, commonly known as "Okies." The camp is the same one described in author John Steinbeck's *The Grapes of Wrath*.

"...the feeling of rejection was greatest among Okie children."

FIRST READ

From Chapter Four: Okie, Go Home!

1   When they left Weedpatch Camp to find work, the Okies faced ridicule, **rejection,** and shame. "Okie use' ta mean you was from Oklahoma," an Okie says in *The Grapes of Wrath*. "Now it means . . . you're scum." A store owner in nearby Arvin called Okies "ignorant, filthy people." A local doctor said they were **"shiftless** trash who lived like dogs." One woman screamed, "There's more darn 'Okies' in California than white people," while a local newspaper, the *Kern Herald,* alarmed readers with the headline MIGRANT HORDE INVADES KERN.

2   Californians were hostile to Okies because they competed with residents for jobs and because taxpayers were forced to pay for problems that arose as a result of the Okie migration to California. For example, **epidemics** of disease in the Okievilles caused the health and **sanitation** budget for Kern County to double between 1935 and 1940. During the same period, overcrowding in the schools caused Kern County's education bill to increase by 214 percent, while property taxes rose 50 percent.

. . .

3   But the feeling of rejection was greatest among Okie children. Because they had been poor for so long and had been traveling for months to get to California, the Okie children had not been able to attend school, and many couldn't read or write. When they went to school each day, most of the teachers ignored the migrants, believing that Okie kids were too stupid to learn the alphabet, too dumb to master math . . . Other teachers forced the newcomers to sit on the floor in the back of the classroom, while the non-Okie kids, well dressed with clean faces and the best school supplies, sat at desks and poked fun at their classmates who wore dresses made out of

chicken-feed sacks, baggy overalls held up by rope, and frequently no shoes at all.

...

From Chapter 5: Mr. Hart

4   Leo Hart liked to visit the Okie children when they played in the field next to Weedpatch Camp. He was forty years old at the time, but it did not seem unusual to the children that this tall, slender man came to their makeshift playground at least once a week. When he played tag or baseball with the Okie kids or sat in a circle with them in the field and talked, the children called him Mr. Hart. He was a caring man who always had a smile on his face, as if he knew some great secret no one else knew.

...

5   The **opposition** to the Okie children angered Leo. Edna Hart recalled that her husband would come home from work so upset that he couldn't eat or sleep. "I could never understand," Leo said, "why these kids should be treated differently. I could never understand why they shouldn't be given the same opportunity as others. Someone had to do something for them because no one cared about them."

6   In 1940 Leo decided that if no one wanted the Okie kids in the public schools, then maybe the Okie children should have their own school. It would be a different school, he thought. It would be more than bricks and buildings, more than lessons and homework in math and writing. It would teach practical skills, such as masonry, mechanics, and agriculture. It would also teach the children to be proud of who they were. It would instill self-confidence in them so they might succeed in life of their own. It would provide the Okie children, Leo said, "with educational experiences in a broader and richer curriculum than were present in most schools." Above all else, Leo insisted, it would be "their school."

From Chapter Six: Weedpatch School

7   In April 1940 Superintendent Hart phoned the president of the Vineland school board, who was usually hostile to Okies and to the superintendent's office. But on this day Leo was phoning to tell the school board just what it wanted to hear.

8   Leo told the president of the board that he wanted to remove the Okie children from the public school. The president enthusiastically agreed. Then Leo asked him to declare that an emergency existed. "The emergency," Leo said, "was overcrowding in the public schools." Knowing that the president

was willing to consider any idea that might solve what he thought of as the Okie problem, Leo asked him for permission to build an "emergency school" for Okie children "at no expense to the district." Swiftly the president granted permission—without asking where the school might be located or how it might come about.

""Okie, Go Home!" (Chapter Four)," "Mr. Hart (Chapter Five)," and "Weedpatch School (Chapter Six)" from CHILDREN OF THE DUST BOWL by Jerry Stanley, copyright © 1992 by Jerry Stanley. Used by permission of Crown Publishers, an imprint of Random House Children's Books, a division of Random House LLC. All rights reserved.

THINK QUESTIONS

1. Write two or three sentences explaining why Californians were hostile toward "Okies." Support your answer with textual evidence.

2. Refer to one or more details from the text to explain how these children were treated in school—both from ideas that are directly stated and ideas that you have inferred from clues in the text.

3. Use details from the text to write two or three sentences describing how Leo Hart was different from other teachers.

4. Use context to determine the meaning of the word **rejection** as it is used in *Children of the Dust Bowl: The True Story of the School at Weedpatch Camp*. Write your definition of "rejection" and tell how you got it. Then, check your definition by using it in the context of a sentence or by looking in a dictionary.

5. Remembering that the Latin root *sanitas* means "health," use this information and the context to determine the meaning of the word **sanitation** as it is used in *Children of the Dust Bowl: The True Story of the School at Weedpatch Camp*. Write your definition of "sanitation" and tell how you got it. Then, check your definition by using it in the context of a sentence or by looking in a dictionary.

STUDYSYNC LIBRARY | Children of the Dust Bowl

CLOSE READ

Reread the excerpt from *Children of the Dust Bowl: The True Story of the School at Weedpatch Camp*. As you reread, complete the Focus Questions below. Then use your answers and annotations from the questions to help you complete the Writing Prompt.

FOCUS QUESTIONS

1. In paragraph 3, the author makes a distinction between "Okie" and "non-Okie" kids. Discuss how the term "Okie" transforms from a neutral word meaning "someone from Oklahoma" (paragraph 1) to a negative word. Highlight textual evidence and make annotations to explain your ideas.

2. The camp in the text, based near Arvin, California, takes on the name "Weedpatch Camp." Based on paragraphs 2 and 3, make annotations about the denotation and connotation of the word "weedpatch" as it is used in the name of the camp. Support your response with textual evidence, and make annotations to explain your ideas.

3. In paragraph 4, author Jerry Stanley describes Leo Hart as "a caring man who always had a smile on his face, as if he knew some great secret no one else knew." What do you think is the author's point of view toward Leo Hart? How does Stanley use word choice to reveal this point of view? Support your response with textual evidence, and make annotations to explain your response.

4. Use the central idea and the most important supporting details from paragraphs 7 and 8 to provide a summary of Leo Hart's plan. Highlight evidence from the text and make annotations to explain your ideas.

5. How did Leo Hart's vision for an "Okie school" show that he was standing up for others? Highlight evidence from the text and make annotations to explain your ideas.

WRITING PROMPT

What is the excerpt from *Children of the Dust Bowl: The True Story of the School at Weedpatch Camp* all about? What do the details in the text have in common? Use your understanding of a central (or main) idea and the details that support the central idea to write an objective summary of the text in your own words. Support your writing with textual evidence. Be sure not to include your feelings, opinions, or judgments in your summary.

THE CIRCUIT:
STORIES FROM THE LIFE OF A MIGRANT CHILD

FICTION
Francisco Jimenez
1997

INTRODUCTION

When Francisco Jimenez was four years old, he and his family immigrated to the United States. At the age of six, he began working on farms, like other members of his family. Now a professor of literature at Santa Clara University in California, Jimenez said, "I came to realize that learning and knowledge were the only stable things in my life. Whatever I learned in school, that knowledge would stay with me no matter how many times we moved." *The Circuit: Stories from the Life of a Migrant Child* is Jimenez's autobiographical novel about migrant farm workers in 1950s California. It describes how migrant workers would go from farm to farm picking fruits and vegetables—also known as travelling the circuit.

"... everything we owned was neatly packed in cardboard boxes."

 FIRST READ

From the Chapter: The Circuit

1. It was that time of year again. Ito, the strawberry sharecropper, did not smile. It was natural. The peak of the strawberry season was over and the last few days the workers, most of them *braceros,* were not picking as many boxes as they had during the months of June and July.

2. As the last days of August disappeared, so did the number of braceros. Sunday, only one—the best picker—came to work. I liked him. Sometimes we talked during our half-hour lunch break. That is how I found out he was from Jalisco, the same state in Mexico my family was from. That Sunday was the last time I saw him.

3. When the sun had tired and sunk behind the mountains, Ito signaled us that it was time to go home. "*Ya esora,*" he yelled in his broken Spanish. Those were the words I waited for twelve hours a day, every day, seven days a week, week after week. And the thought of not hearing them again saddened me.

4. As we drove home Papá did not say a word. With both hands on the wheel, he stared at the dirt road. My older brother, Roberto, was also silent. He leaned his head back and closed his eyes. Once in a while he cleared from his throat the dust that blew in from outside.

5. Yes, it was that time of year. When I opened the front door to the shack, I stopped. Everything we owned was neatly packed in cardboard boxes. Suddenly I felt even more the weight of hours, days, weeks, and months of work. I sat down on a box. The thought of having to move to Fresno and knowing what was in store for me there brought tears to my eyes.

6   That night I could not sleep. I lay in bed thinking about how much I hated this move.

7   A little before five o'clock in the morning, Papá woke everyone up. A few minutes later, the yelling and screaming of my little brothers and sisters, for whom the move was a great adventure, broke the silence of dawn. Shortly, the barking of the dogs accompanied them.

8   While we packed the breakfast dishes, Papá went outside to start the "*Carcachita.*" That was the name Papá gave his old black Plymouth. He bought it in a used-car lot in Santa Rosa. Papá was very proud of his little jalopy. He had a right to be proud of it. He spent a lot of time looking at other cars before buying this one. When he finally chose the *Carcachita,* he checked it thoroughly before driving it out of the car lot. He examined every inch of the car. He listened to the motor, tilting his head from side to side like a parrot, trying to **detect** any noises that spelled car trouble. After being satisfied with the looks and sounds of the car, Papá then insisted on knowing who the original owner was. He never did find out from the car salesman, but he bought the car anyway. Papá figured the original owner must have been an important man because behind the rear seat of the car he found a blue necktie.

9   Papá parked the car out in front and left the motor running. "*Listo,*" he yelled. Without saying a word, Roberto and I began to carry the boxes out to the car. Roberto carried the two big boxes and I carried the two smaller ones. Papá then threw the mattress on top of the car roof and tied it with ropes to the front and rear bumpers.

10 Everything was packed except Mamá's pot. It was on old large galvanized pot she had picked up at an army surplus store in Santa Maria. The pot had many dents and nicks, and the more dents and nicks it **acquired** the more Mamá liked it. "*Mi olla,*" she used to say proudly.

11 I held the front door open as Mamá carefully carried out her pot by both handles, making sure not to spill the cooked beans. When she got to the car, Papá reached out to help her with it. Roberto opened the rear car door and Papá gently placed it on the floor behind the front seat. All of us then climbed in. Papá sighed, wiped the sweat off his forehead with his sleeve, and said wearily: "*Es todo.*"

12 As we drove away, I felt a lump in my throat. I turned around and looked at our little shack for the last time.

13 At sunset we drove into a labor camp near Fresno. Since Papá did not speak English, Mamá asked the camp **foreman** if he needed any more workers. "We don't need no more," said the foreman, scratching his head. "Check with

Sullivan down the road. Can't miss him. He lives in a big white house with a fence around it."

14 When we got there, Mamá walked up to the house. She went through a white gate, past a row of rose bushes, up the stairs to the front door. She rang the doorbell. The porch light went on and tall husky man came out. They exchanged a few words. After the man went in, Mamá clasped her hands and hurried back to the car. "We have work! Mr. Sullivan said we can stay there the whole season," she said, gasping and pointing to an old garage near the stables.

15 The garage was worn out by the years. It had no windows. The walls, eaten by termites, strained to support the roof full of holes. The dirt floor, populated by earthworms, looked like a gray road map.

16 That night, by the light of a kerosene lamp, we unpacked and cleaned our new home. Roberto swept away the loose dirt, leaving the hard ground. Papá plugged the holes in the walls with old newspapers and tin can tops. Mamá fed my little brothers and sisters. Papá and Roberto then brought in the mattress and placed it on the far corner of the garage. "Mamá, you and the little ones sleep on the mattress. Roberto, Panchito, and I will sleep outside under the trees," Papá said.

17 Early next morning Mr. Sullivan showed us where his crop was, and after breakfast, Papá, Roberto, and I headed for the vineyard to pick.

18 Around nine o'clock the temperature had risen to almost one hundred degrees. I was completely soaked in sweat and my mouth felt as if I had been chewing on a handkerchief. I walked over to the end of the row, picked up the jug of water we had brought, and began drinking. "Don't drink too much; you'll get sick," Roberto shouted. No sooner had he said that than I felt sick to my stomach. I dropped to my knees and let the jug roll off my hands. I remained motionless with my eyes glued on the hot sandy ground. All I could hear was the drone of insects. Slowly I began to recover. I poured water over my face and neck and watched the dirty water run down my arms to the ground.

19 I still felt a little dizzy when we took a break to eat lunch. It was past two o'clock and we sat underneath a large walnut tree that was on the side of the road. While we ate, Papá jotted down the number of boxes we had picked. Roberto drew designs on the ground with a stick. Suddenly I noticed Papá's face turn pale as he looked down the road. "Here comes the school bus," he whispered loudly in alarm. Instinctively, Roberto and I ran and hid in the vineyards. We did not want to get in trouble for not going to school. The neatly dressed boys about my age got off. They carried books under their

arms. After they crossed the street, the bus drove away. Roberto and I came out from hiding and joined Papá. "*Tienen que tener cuidado,*" he warned us.

20 After lunch we went back to work. The sun kept beating down. The buzzing insects, the wet sweat, and the hot dry dust made the afternoon seem to last forever. Finally the mountains around the valley reached out and swallowed the sun. Within an hour it was too dark to continue picking. The vines blanketed the grapes, making it difficult to see the bunches. "*Vámanos,*" said Papá, signaling to us that it was time to quit work. Papá then took out a pencil and began to figure out how much we had earned our first day. He wrote down numbers, crossed some out, wrote down some more, "*Quince,*" he murmured.

21 When we arrived home, we took a cold shower underneath a water hose. We then sat down to eat dinner around some wooden crates that served as a table. Mamá had cooked a special meal for us. We had rice and tortillas with *carne con chile,* my favorite dish.

22 The next morning I could hardly move. My body ached all over. I felt little control over my arms and legs. This feeling went on every morning for days until my muscles finally got used to the work.

23 It was Monday, the first week of November. The grape season was over and I could now go to school. I woke up early that morning and lay in bed, looking at the stars and **savoring** the thought of not going to work and of starting sixth grade for the first time that year. Since I could not sleep, I decided to get up and join Papá and Roberto at breakfast. I sat at the table across from Roberto, but I kept my head down. I did not want to look up and face him. I knew he was sad. He was not going to school today. He was not going tomorrow, or next week, or next month. He would not go until the cotton season was over, and that was sometime in February. I rubbed my hands together and watched the dry, acid stained skin fall to the floor in little rolls.

24 When Papá and Roberto left for work, I felt relief. I walked to the top of a small grade next to the shack and watched the *Carcachita* disappear in the distance in a cloud of dust.

25 Two hours later, around eight o'clock, I stood by the side of the road waiting for school bus number twenty. When it arrived I climbed in. Everyone was busy either talking or yelling. I sat in an empty seat in the back.

26 When the bus stopped in front of the school, I felt very nervous. I looked out the bus window and saw boys and girls carrying books under their arms. I put my hands in my pant pockets and walked to the principal's office. When I entered I heard a woman's voice say: "May I help you?" I was startled. I had not heard English for months. For a few seconds I remained speechless. I

looked at the lady who waited for an answer. My first instinct was to answer her in Spanish, but I held back. Finally, after struggling for English words, I managed to tell her that I wanted to enroll in the sixth grade. After answering many questions, I was led to the classroom.

27 Mr. Lema, the sixth grade teacher, greeted me and assigned me a desk. He then introduced me to the class. I was so nervous and scared at that moment when everyone's eyes were on me that I wished I were with Papá and Roberto picking cotton. After taking roll, Mr. Lema gave the class the assignment for the first hour. "The first thing we have to do this morning is finish reading the story we began yesterday," he said enthusiastically. He walked up to me, handed me an English book, and asked me to read. "We are on page 125," he said politely. When I heard this, I felt my blood rush to my head; I felt dizzy. "Would you like to read?" he asked **hesitantly**. I opened the book to page 125. My mouth was dry. My eyes began to water. I could not begin. "You can read later," Mr. Lema said understandingly.

28 For the rest of the reading period I kept getting angrier and angrier with myself. I should have read, I thought to myself. During recess I went into the restroom and opened my English book to page 125. I began to read in a low voice, pretending I was in class. There were many words I did not know. I closed the book and headed back to the classroom.

29 Mr. Lema was sitting at his desk correcting papers. When I entered he looked up at me and smiled. I felt better. I walked up to him and asked if he could help me with the new words. "Gladly," he said.

30 The rest of the month I spent my lunch hours working on English with Mr. Lema, my best friend at school.

31 One Friday, during lunch hour, Mr. Lema asked me to take a walk with him to the music room. "Do you like music?" he asked me as we entered the building. "Yes, I like *corridos*," I answered. He then picked up a trumpet, blew on it, and handed it to me. The sound gave me goose bumps. I knew that sound. I had heard it in many *corridos*. "How would you like to learn how to play it?" he asked. He must have read my face because before I could answer, he added: "I'll teach you how to play it during our lunch hours."

32 That day I could hardly wait to tell Papá and Mamá the great news. As I got off the bus, my little brothers and sisters ran up to meet me. They were yelling and screaming. I thought they were happy to see me, but when I opened the door to our shack, I saw that everything we owned was neatly packed in cardboard boxes.

STUDYSYNC LIBRARY | **The Circuit: Stories From the Life of a Migrant Child**

© 1992 by Francisco Jimenez, THE CIRCUIT: STORIES FROM THE LIFE OF A MIGRANT CHILD. Reproduced by permission of Francisco Jimenez.

 THINK QUESTIONS

1. How does Francisco feel about moving from farm to farm? Support your response with details that are directly stated in the story and ideas that you infer.

2. In what ways are Francisco's feelings about school divided? What causes this? Support your response with textual evidence from the story.

3. Use textual evidence to describe the role that Mr. Lema plays in Francisco's life, as well as how Francisco is affected by him.

4. Use context to determine the meaning of the word **foreman** as it is used in *The Circuit: Stories From the Life of a Migrant Child*. Write your definition of "foreman" and tell how you got it.

5. Use context to determine the meaning of the word **savoring** as it is used in *The Circuit: Stories From the Life of a Migrant Child*. Write your definition of "savoring" and tell how you got it.

STUDYSYNC LIBRARY | The Circuit: Stories From the Life of a Migrant Child

CLOSE READ

Reread the excerpt from *The Circuit: Stories From the Life of a Migrant Child*. As you reread, complete the Focus Questions below. Then use your answers and annotations from the questions to help you complete the Writing Prompt.

FOCUS QUESTIONS

1. In paragraph 8, Francisco describes Papá's car and tells readers the story of how Papá bought it. How does this description help you get to know Papá from Francisco's perspective? Highlight details in the paragraph that help you infer Papá's character traits, and make annotations to record your ideas.

2. In paragraph 27, Francisco meets his sixth grade teacher, Mr. Lema. Highlight textual evidence in this paragraph that indicates Francisco's impression of his teacher. Then make annotations to explain how this viewpoint supports the actions Francisco takes in the next two paragraphs.

3. In both paragraph 5 and the final paragraph, Francisco comes home to find his family's belongings "neatly packed in cardboard boxes." Why do you think he specifically uses the word "neatly" each time he describes this detail to readers? How does this description contrast with Francisco's feelings about moving? Annotate your ideas and highlight evidence from the text that supports them.

4. In the last two paragraphs, how does the mood, or emotional feeling of the story, change to reflect what Francisco is now feeling? Annotate your ideas and highlight evidence from the text that supports them.

5. In what ways does the use of first-person point of view allow readers to better understand the challenges Francisco faces in *The Circuit*? In what ways might a third-person point of view give readers a different understanding of these challenges? Annotate your ideas and highlight evidence from the text that supports them.

WRITING PROMPT

Author Francisco Jimenez chose to write his autobiographical novel *The Circuit: Stories from the Life of a Migrant Child* from the first-person point of view of a child migrant worker.

How might the story be different if told from the point of view of Francisco's mother or father? What might the reader discover about his parents' thoughts and feelings as they anticipate another move? Examine and explain how changing the point of view from the boy to one of his parents might reveal different aspects of what life was like for migrant workers as they faced challenges and hardships. Remember to support your central idea with relevant, well-organized evidence from the text, including quotations, details, and examples, to show how the point of view in a story influences readers' understanding of characters and their experiences.

LES MISÉRABLES

FICTION
Victor Hugo
1862

INTRODUCTION

studysync

Victor Hugo's *Les Misérables*, set during the turbulent years after Napoleon's defeat in the early 19th Century, is the dramatic story of Jean Valjean. Valjean has spent nineteen years in prison for stealing a loaf of bread to feed his sister's family and then for numerous escape attempts. When he is at last released from prison, he is marked as an ex-convict, facing a hostile world and forced to sleep on the street. Finally, embittered and losing his spirit, he is given refuge by the good-natured Bishop Myriel, known as Monseigneur Bienvenu for his welcoming nature. Valjean has now come to a crossroads where he will face a moral challenge that will change his life and those around him forever.

"Jean Valjean, my brother, you no longer belong to evil, but to good."

FIRST READ

Excerpt from Chapter V

TRANQUILITY

1. After bidding his sister good night, Monseigneur Bienvenu took one of the two silver candlesticks from the table, handed the other to his guest, and said to him, —

2. "Monsieur, I will conduct you to your room."

3. The man followed him.

4. As might have been observed from what has been said above, the house was so arranged that in order to pass into the oratory where the alcove was situated, or to get out of it, it was necessary to traverse the Bishop's bedroom.

5. At the moment when he was crossing this apartment, Madame Magloire was putting away the silverware in the cupboard near the head of the bed. This was her last care every evening before she went to bed.

6. The Bishop installed his guest in the alcove. A fresh white bed had been prepared there. The man set the candle down on a small table.

7. "Well," said the Bishop, "may you pass a good night. To-morrow morning, before you set out, you shall drink a cup of warm milk from our cows."

8. "Thanks, Monsieur l'Abbe," said the man.

9. Hardly had he pronounced these words full of peace, when all of a sudden, and without transition, he made a strange movement, which would have frozen the two sainted women with horror, had they witnessed it. Even at this

day it is difficult for us to explain what inspired him at that moment. Did he intend to convey a warning or to throw out a menace? Was he simply obeying a sort of instinctive impulse which was obscure even to himself? He turned abruptly to the old man, folded his arms, and bending upon his host a savage gaze, he exclaimed in a hoarse voice:—

10   "Ah! really! You lodge me in your house, close to yourself like this?"

11   He broke off, and added with a laugh in which there lurked something monstrous:—

12   "Have you really reflected well? How do you know that I have not been an assassin?"

13   The Bishop replied:—

14   "That is the concern of the good God."

15   Then gravely, and moving his lips like one who is praying or talking to himself, he raised two fingers of his right hand and bestowed his **benediction** on the man, who did not bow, and without turning his head or looking behind him, he returned to his bedroom.

Excerpt from Chapter XII

THE BISHOP WORKS

16   The next morning at sunrise Monseigneur Bienvenu was strolling in his garden. Madame Magloire ran up to him in utter consternation.

17   "Monseigneur, Monseigneur!" she exclaimed, "does your Grace know where the basket of silver is?"

18   "Yes," replied the Bishop.

19   "Jesus the Lord be blessed!" she resumed; "I did not know what had become of it."

20   The Bishop had just picked up the basket in a flower-bed. He presented it to Madame Magloire.

21   "Here it is."

22   "Well!" said she. "Nothing in it! And the silver?"

23   "Ah," returned the Bishop, "so it is the silver which troubles you? I don't know where it is."

24 "Great, good God! It is stolen! That man who was here last night has stolen it."

25 In a twinkling, with all the vivacity of an alert old woman, Madame Magloire had rushed to the oratory, entered the alcove, and returned to the Bishop. The Bishop had just bent down, and was sighing as he examined a plant of cochlearia des Guillons, which the basket had broken as it fell across the bed. He rose up at Madame Magloire's cry.

26 "Monseigneur, the man is gone! The silver has been stolen!"

27 As she uttered this exclamation, her eyes fell upon a corner of the garden, where traces of the wall having been scaled were visible. The coping of the wall had been torn away.

28 "Stay! yonder is the way he went. He jumped over into Cochefilet Lane. Ah, the abomination! He has stolen our silver!"

29 The Bishop remained silent for a moment; then he raised his grave eyes, and said gently to Madame Magloire:—

30 "And, in the first place, was that silver ours?"

31 Madame Magloire was speechless. Another silence ensued; then the Bishop went on:—

32 "Madame Magloire, I have for a long time detained that silver wrongfully. It belonged to the poor. Who was that man? A poor man, evidently."

33 "Alas! Jesus!" returned Madame Magloire. "It is not for my sake, nor for Mademoiselle's. It makes no difference to us. But it is for the sake of Monseigneur. What is Monseigneur to eat with now?"

34 The Bishop gazed at her with an air of amazement.

35 "Ah, come! Are there no such things as pewter forks and spoons?"

36 Madame Magloire shrugged her shoulders.

37 "Pewter has an odor."

38 "Iron forks and spoons, then."

39 Madame Magloire made an expressive grimace.

40 "Iron has a taste."

41 "Very well," said the Bishop; "wooden ones then."

42 A few moments later he was breakfasting at the very table at which Jean Valjean had sat on the previous evening. As he ate his breakfast, Monseigneur Welcome remarked gayly to his sister, who said nothing, and to Madame Magloire, who was grumbling under her breath, that one really does not need either fork or spoon, even of wood, in order to dip a bit of bread in a cup of milk.

43 "A pretty idea, truly," said Madame Magloire to herself, as she went and came, "to take in a man like that! and to lodge him close to one's self! And how fortunate that he did nothing but steal! Ah, mon Dieu! it makes one shudder to think of it!"

44 As the brother and sister were about to rise from the table, there came a knock at the door.

45 "Come in," said the Bishop.

46 The door opened. A singular and violent group made its appearance on the threshold. Three men were holding a fourth man by the collar. The three men were gendarmes; the other was Jean Valjean.

47 A brigadier of gendarmes, who seemed to be in command of the group, was standing near the door. He entered and advanced to the Bishop, making a military salute.

48 "Monseigneur—" said he.

49 At this word, Jean Valjean, who was dejected and seemed overwhelmed, raised his head with an air of **stupefaction.**

50 "Monseigneur!" he murmured. "So he is not the cure?"

51 "Silence!" said the gendarme. "He is Monseigneur the Bishop."

52 In the meantime, Monseigneur Bienvenu had advanced as quickly as his great age permitted.

53 "Ah! here you are!" he exclaimed, looking at Jean Valjean. "I am glad to see you. Well, but how is this? I gave you the candlesticks too, which are of silver like the rest, and for which you can certainly get two hundred francs. Why did you not carry them away with your forks and spoons?"

54 Jean Valjean opened his eyes wide, and stared at the **venerable** Bishop with an expression which no human tongue can render any account of.

55 "Monseigneur," said the brigadier of gendarmes, "so what this man said is true, then? We came across him. He was walking like a man who is running away. We stopped him to look into the matter. He had this silver—"

56 "And he told you," interposed the Bishop with a smile, "that it had been given to him by a kind old fellow of a priest with whom he had passed the night? I see how the matter stands. And you have brought him back here? It is a mistake."

57 "In that case," replied the brigadier, "we can let him go?"

58 "Certainly," replied the Bishop.

59 The gendarmes released Jean Valjean, who recoiled.

60 "Is it true that I am to be released?" he said, in an almost inarticulate voice, and as though he were talking in his sleep.

61 "Yes, thou art released; dost thou not understand?" said one of the gendarmes.

62 "My friend," resumed the Bishop, "before you go, here are your candlesticks. Take them."

63 He stepped to the chimney-piece, took the two silver candlesticks, and brought them to Jean Valjean. The two women looked on without uttering a word, without a gesture, without a look which could disconcert the Bishop.

64 Jean Valjean was trembling in every limb. He took the two candlesticks mechanically, and with a bewildered air.

65 "Now," said the Bishop, "go in peace. By the way, when you return, my friend, it is not necessary to pass through the garden. You can always enter and depart through the street door."

66 Then, turning to the gendarmes:—

67 "You may retire, gentlemen."

68 The gendarmes retired.

69 Jean Valjean was like a man on the point of fainting.

70 The Bishop drew near to him, and said in a low voice:—

71 "Do not forget, never forget, that you have promised to use this money in becoming an honest man."

72 Jean Valjean, who had no recollection of ever having promised anything, remained speechless. The Bishop had emphasized the words when he uttered them. He resumed with solemnity:—

73 "Jean Valjean, my brother, you no longer belong to evil, but to good. It is your soul that I buy from you; I withdraw it from black thoughts and the spirit of **perdition,** and I give it to God."

74 It is never fastened with anything but a latch, either by day or by night."

THINK QUESTIONS

1. How does Jean Valjean react when the Bishop wishes him a good night and tells him that he'll be given a cup of warm milk in the morning? How does the Bishop respond to what Valjean says? Support your answers with textual evidence.

2. How does Valjean repay the Bishop's kindness the next morning? Support your answer with textual evidence.

3. How does the Bishop respond to Valjean's return? Support your answer both with evidence that is directly stated and with ideas that you have inferred from clues in the text.

4. The Latin root *vener-* (or *venus*) means "love" or "charm." The affix *-able* means "capable of" or "fit for." Use this, along with context clues from the text, to determine the meaning of the word **venerable** as it is used in *Les Misérables*. Write your definition of "venerable" and tell how you determined it.

5. Remembering that the Latin root *bene* means "well" and the root *dict* means "to speak," use the context clues provided in the passage to determine the meaning of benediction. Write your definition of **"benediction"** and tell how you determined it

CLOSE READ

Reread the excerpt from *Les Misérables*. As you reread, complete the Focus Questions below. Then use your answers and annotations from the questions to help you complete the Writing Prompt.

FOCUS QUESTIONS

1. After the Bishop wishes his guest good night, Valjean responds first in one way, and then in a completely different way. What do his two very different responses tell you about Valjean's character? What clues can you find in his responses that contribute to the development of the story's theme? Highlight and annotate textual evidence to support your answers.

2. Following Valjean's implied threat about having been an assassin, how does the Bishop respond? What does the Bishop's response tell you both about his character and about his view of the purpose and function of the church? Highlight and annotate textual evidence to explain your answers and inferences.

3. After Madame Magloire discovers that the silver is missing, the Bishop says, "I have for a long time detained that silver wrongfully. It belonged to the poor. Who was that man? A poor man, evidently." Why do you think the Bishop feels that he has "detained that silver wrongfully"? What clues can you find in his statement that contribute to the development of the story's theme? Highlight and annotate evidence from the text to support your answers.

4. How does Madame Magloire feel about what Valjean does, and about what the Bishop does? What clues to the story's theme can you find in her attitude and responses? Highlight evidence from the text and make annotations to support your views of Madame Magloire.

5. Valjean accepts the silver candlesticks from the Bishop. With this action, does Valjean agree to the promise that the Bishop warns him never to forget? Will he accept the Bishop's challenge? Highlight evidence from the text and make annotations to support your response.

WRITING PROMPT

The Bishop, who sees goodness in Valjean and wants him to lead an honest life, implies to the gendarmes that Valjean did not steal the silver. Does his wish to help Valjean, to stand up for him, justify what he tells the gendarmes? What other reasons might he have had for acting as he does? Write a brief essay explaining how the Bishop's words and actions in relation to Valjean, particularly in the presence of the gendarmes, help reveal the story's theme. Use relevant, well-organized textual evidence to develop your ideas.

JABBERWOCKY

POETRY
Lewis Carroll
1872

INTRODUCTION

studysync

This whimsical poem about a heroic quest was first published in its entirety in author Lewis Carroll's *Through the Looking Glass*. Alice finds the poem in a book after she steps through the mirror into an odd new world. The poem's fantastical characters, invented language and formal structure have made it a classic in its own right.

"Beware the Jabberwock, my son!"

FIRST READ

From Chapter 1: "Looking-Glass House"

1. 'Twas brillig, and the slithy toves
2. Did gyre and gimble in the wabe;
3. All mimsy were the borogoves,
4. And the mome raths outgrabe.

5. 'Beware the Jabberwock, my son!
6. The jaws that bite, the claws that catch!
7. Beware the Jubjub bird, and **shun**
8. The frumious Bandersnatch!'

9. He took his vorpal sword in hand:
10. Long time the manxome foe he **sought**—
11. So rested he by the Tumtum tree,
12. And stood awhile in thought.

13. And as in uffish thought he stood,
14. The Jabberwock, with eyes of flame,
15. Came whiffling through the tulgey wood,
16. And **burbled** as it came!

17. One, two! One, two! And through and through
18. The vorpal blade went snicker-snack!
19. He left it dead, and with its head
20. He went **galumphing** back.

21. 'And hast thou slain the Jabberwock?
22. Come to my arms, my beamish boy!

STUDYSYNC LIBRARY | Jabberwocky

23 O frabjous day! Callooh! Callay!'
24 He **chortled** in his joy.

25 'Twas brillig, and the slithy toves
26 Did gyre and gimble in the wabe;
27 All mimsy were the borogoves,
28 And the mome raths out grabe.

THINK QUESTIONS

1. The person who kills the Jabberwock is related to the narrator of the poem. What is the relationship? Cite textual evidence for your answer.

2. What do you think the Jabberwock looks like? Use details from the text to write two or three sentences describing the Jabberwock.

3. Summarize the action of "Jabberwocky." For each major event, provide a piece of evidence from the text.

4. Use context to determine the meaning of the word **shun** as it is used in *Jabberwocky*. Write your definition of "shun" and tell how you found it. Then, consult a dictionary to check your definition. What is the precise meaning of "shun"?

5. Use the context clues provided in the passage to determine the meaning of **galumphing.** Write your definition of "galumphing" and tell how you got it. How do you think this word might sound aloud? Then, using a dictionary or similar resource, check your definition and determine the correct pronunciation of "galumphing."

STUDYSYNC LIBRARY | Jabberwocky

CLOSE READ

Reread the poem "Jabberwocky." As you reread, complete the Focus Questions below. Then use your answers and annotations from the questions to help you complete the Writing Prompt.

FOCUS QUESTIONS

1. How does the poet's use of invented words in the first stanza affect the tone of the poem? Annotate the text to cite specific words and phrases as evidence of the poem's tone.

2. In "Jabberwocky," much of the fun is that a heroic adventure is described in a silly way. From the first four stanzas, highlight two examples of descriptions that use a heroic tone and a silly tone at the same time. Annotate the text with a note about how the words you highlighted contribute to the tone.

3. Many of the words that Lewis Carroll invented for this poem sound like what they seem to mean. This is called *onomatopoeia*. From the last four stanzas of the poem, highlight two words from the poem that sound like what you think they mean. Annotate the text to provide the meaning that you infer, and explain how the sound helped you find the meaning.

4. The final stanza is exactly the same as the first stanza. Highlight these stanzas and make annotations about how you think this affects the tone of the poem. Include an annotation about how you would read these two stanzas and the tone of voice you would use. Describe any differences between how you would read the first and last stanzas and refer to specific words and phrases in the text.

5. How does the young man in "Jabberwocky" stand up for himself? What effects does his action have? Highlight the text that shows evidence of this.

WRITING PROMPT

What serious point do you think Lewis Carroll might be making in "Jabberwocky"? Use your understanding of tone and connotation to support your opinion. Cite evidence from the text to develop your claim about the more serious meaning of "Jabberwocky."

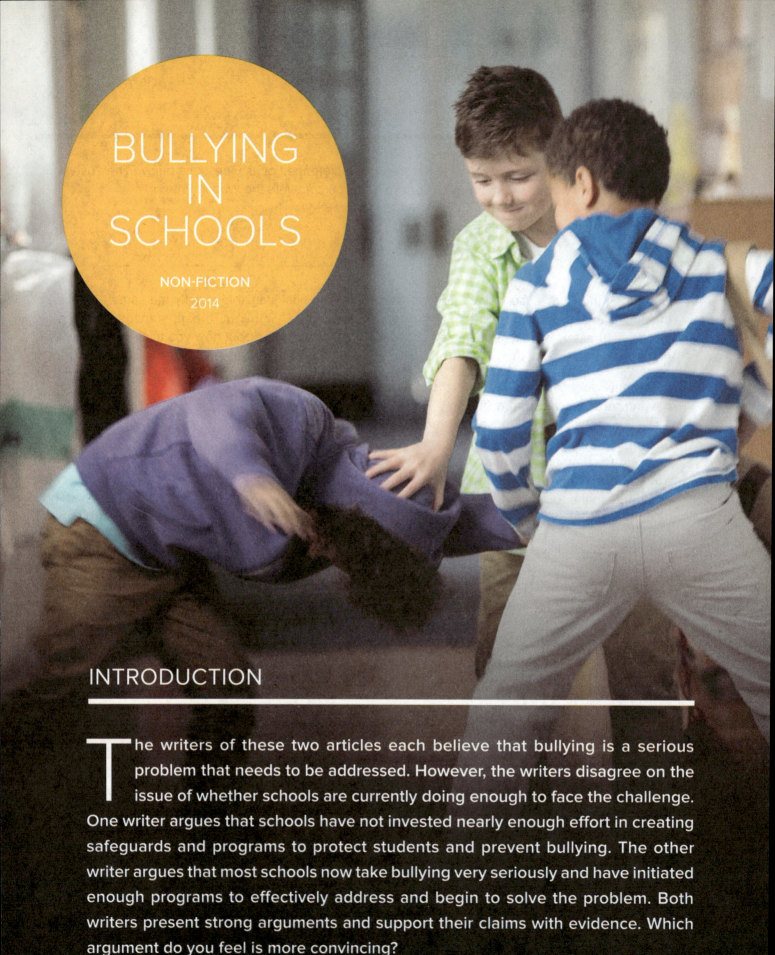

BULLYING IN SCHOOLS

NON-FICTION
2014

INTRODUCTION

The writers of these two articles each believe that bullying is a serious problem that needs to be addressed. However, the writers disagree on the issue of whether schools are currently doing enough to face the challenge. One writer argues that schools have not invested nearly enough effort in creating safeguards and programs to protect students and prevent bullying. The other writer argues that most schools now take bullying very seriously and have initiated enough programs to effectively address and begin to solve the problem. Both writers present strong arguments and support their claims with evidence. Which argument do you feel is more convincing?

"...one of three students is bullied either in school or through social media."

FIRST READ

1. **Bullying in Schools: Are We Doing Enough?**

2. **Point: Schools Are Not Doing Enough to Prevent Bullying**

3. Although the media continues to raise public awareness of student bullying, many schools are still not doing enough to face the challenge of solving the problem. Most teachers and school administrators do not witness bullying. Sometimes they don't know how to recognize it. Sometimes they ignore it. They may also hold the age-old attitude that bullying is just something children do or go through. They think it's a normal part of growing up. But we know now that the repercussions of bullying can be lasting and severe. Sometimes they even end in tragedy.

4. The simple fact that a huge amount of bullying still happens demonstrates that not enough is being done about the issue. The exact number of victims is hard to determine because many incidents go unreported. The National Center for Education Statistics reported in 2013 that one of three students is bullied either in school or through social media. This statistic includes both physical and emotional harassment. Either form can leave lasting scars on victims. Students who are bullied often become very stressed. They can have trouble sleeping and begin to do poorly in school. Furthermore, victims are at a greater risk of suffering from low self-esteem, anxiety, and depression. These effects can even continue well into adulthood.

5. One way in which schools are failing to keep pace with the problem is in adequately supervising school property. Bullying usually happens in unsupervised areas like bathrooms, cafeterias, and school buses. The simplest solution would be for schools to put teachers, monitors, or aides in these areas. Unfortunately, many schools do not have enough staff to ensure that these areas are supervised.

6. An even harder venue to monitor for bullying is the Internet. Cyber-bullying, or bullying that happens over social media, is often extremely hard to track. It is easy to delete comments or pictures before authority figures can see them. In many cases there is little evidence to go on. Students, teachers, and administrators all need to be educated about how to deal with the challenge of cyber-bullying. There are not currently enough programs that address this issue.

7. Most schools also do not have a clear procedure or policy for investigating bullying. This means that if a victim is brave enough to come forward and ask for help, he or she often does not receive it. This is because administrators and authorities do not have a set path for examining the situation. They do not have a plan for ending harmful situations.

8. In addition to educating teachers and administrators about bullying, schools need more programs to help students themselves address the problem. Top-down approaches that simply dole out punishments for bullies are not enough to solve the problem. Students need to be taught more about the ways their words and actions can hurt others. They also need to learn that cases of bullying are often more complex than a "perpetrator" and a "victim." Often, a situation of perceived "bullying" is actually made up of several smaller events. Different students may have played different roles. A student may be bullied one day and become the bully the next. These complicated interactions and behaviors can make it difficult to find a solution that will satisfy all parties.

9. Many schools have "zero-tolerance" policies regarding bullying. These policies are often not sensitive enough to students' particular needs and reasons for behaving the way they do. Every school is different, and student issues can vary widely. Teachers and administrators need to listen carefully to students' problems and perceived injustices, and be sensitive to them. If a student is punished for being a bully when he or she has a different perspective on the situation, that student may feel unfairly persecuted or "ganged-up on." Casting bullies as one-sided villains can be just as damaging to a student as being bullied.

10. Another issue with these "zero-tolerance" policies is that they can often encourage teachers and administrators to over-discipline students. Sometimes one-time or casual conflicts between students can be blown out of proportion. Students may be punished needlessly.

11. We need more policies and programs in place to educate students, teachers, administrators, and parents about what bullying is and how to recognize it. Policies and programs need to show how to end bullying, and, most importantly, what *causes* it. Most schools that do have anti-bullying strategies only deal with the surface of the problem. They don't address the underlying

causes. Without getting to the root of the situation, the problem of bullying can never truly be solved.

12 **Counterpoint: Most Schools Are Doing Their Best to Stop Bullying**

13 A group of students is playing on the playground. One boy pokes another in the back while waiting in line for the swings. "Knock it off," says the boy. "That's not nice."

14 "Oh, sorry," says the first boy, and stops. "I didn't really mean that."

15 This is the sort of response you might hear on the playground at a school in Forest Lakes, Minnesota, where Dave Seaburg is a teacher. In many schools across the country, bullying is being reduced or eliminated thanks to anti-bullying programs and policies. These programs are carried out by dedicated teachers like Mr. Seaburg. As part of an anti-bullying program, he leads workshops and provides lessons designed to teach students about the harmful effects of bullying. Students also learn ways to empower themselves against it. The school district where Dave Seaburg works has seen a steady decline in bullying since anti-bullying programs were implemented.

16 Schools across the United States are in fact doing an enormous amount to meet the challenge of bullying. As the media has heightened awareness of the issue, the attention devoted to solving the problem has been growing steadily. One example would be schools in the state of New Jersey. The first law against bullying in New Jersey schools was passed by the state legislature a little more than a decade ago. Within a few years, school districts were required to appoint an anti-bullying coordinator in every school. Today, according to the *Asbury Park Press,* each New Jersey school district spends more than thirty thousand dollars a year on supplies, software, additional personnel, and staff and teacher training devoted to anti-bullying measures.

17 How many school districts are expending this kind of effort? Certainly, many hundreds. More than forty-five states currently have laws on the books that direct school districts to adopt anti-bullying programs. Organizations from the National Education Association to the National Association of Student Councils are developing initiatives aimed at preventing bullying.

18 What exactly do school programs to prevent bullying do, and how do they work? There is no one single profile. A New Hampshire law states that all school staff must be trained to know what bullying looks like. People learn to spot the signs, and those who see bullying must report it. In Midland, Texas, police officers visit the schools to let students know that bullying is a crime. A school district in Miami, Florida has implemented several anti-bullying programs including Challenge Day and Girls Day Out. Girls Day Out teachs

girls how they can deal with social issues in a positive way rather than resorting to bullying.

19. When it comes to cyber-bullying, it can be extremely difficult for a school to monitor and police students' activity on social media. Some of the effort needs to be made on the part of the parents. When parents take an active role in their children's social media usage, it becomes much easier to keep track of what's going on. Also, students are less likely to cyber-bully if they know their Internet activity is being supervised and they are being held accountable for their actions. Even in the arena of cyber-bullying, however, there is a role schools can and do play. In more than a dozen states, schools have been authorized to take disciplinary action against students who engage in bullying that takes place off of school property.

20. For example, the state of California recently passed Seth's Law. This new law strengthens the anti-bullying legislation that is already in place. It requires all California public schools to regularly update their anti-bullying programs and policies. There are even provisions for cyber-bullying. Seth's Law also focuses on protecting students who are victims of bullying due to their race, gender, sexual orientation, religion, or disabilities. Seth's Law makes it mandatory for teachers and authority figures to take action against any bullying behavior that they witness.

21. If school anti-bullying programs vary widely, are there any general guidelines that can be recommended? Certainly controversial issues exist where school policies are concerned. Should bullies be suspended or otherwise punished, or should they be helped with counseling and anger management programs? Should bystanders who witness bullying and fail to report it be reprimanded? Should schools be involved at all, or is bullying a family matter, as some people contend?

22. The federal government hosts a website, http://stopbullying.gov, with information for students, parents, and teachers on the issue of bullying. It suggests a number of different measures that schools can implement. For teachers and staff, these measures include finding out why, when, and where bullying takes place; launching awareness campaigns; creating school safety committees; and building information into the student curriculum. The website also recommends something that can be useful everywhere at all times—creating a culture of civility and tolerance.

23. Most schools are doing all they can to raise awareness, prevent, and ultimately eliminate bullying. If they devote any more time to anti-bullying education than they already do, it will take time away from core subjects like math and language arts. Anti-bullying programs are expensive for schools to run and they require highly trained staff.

STUDYSYNC LIBRARY | Bullying in Schools

24. Still, even with the very best anti-bullying programs and policies, it can take a long time for change to come about. It may be as many as three to ten years before an anti-bullying culture becomes standard all over the country. Though it may not seem like schools are doing enough because bullying still persists, even the most effective programs will take time to bring about the sort of change people are looking for.

THINK QUESTIONS

1. Use details from the text to explain the "Point" author's response to the question *Bullying in Schools: Are We Doing Enough?* Cite the "Point" author's main claim and one reason why the author makes the claim. What evidence does the author use to support this position?

2. Use details from the text to explain the "Counterpoint" author's response to the question *Bullying in Schools: Are We Doing Enough?* Cite the "Counterpoint" author's main claim and one reason why the author makes this claim. What evidence does the author use to support this position?

3. The "Point" author acknowledges that some schools have "'zero-tolerance' policies," but he or she is critical of them. Explain why the author takes issue with these policies. Use textual evidence to support your answer.

4. Use context to determine the meaning of the word **venue** as it is used in "Bullying in Schools." Write your definition of "venue" and tell how you determined its meaning. Then, check your inferred definition both in context and with a dictionary.

5. Remembering that the suffix or means "person connected with," use the context clues provided in the selection to determine the meaning of **perpetrator.** Write your definition of "perpetrator" and tell how you determined its meaning. Plug your inferred meaning into the original sentence to check it, and then consult a dictionary to confirm your meaning.

STUDYSYNC LIBRARY | Bullying in Schools

CLOSE READ

Reread the Point/Counterpoint debate "Bullying in Schools." As you reread, complete the Focus Questions below. Then use your answers and annotations from the questions to help you complete the Writing Prompt.

FOCUS QUESTIONS

1. The introductory first paragraph of the "Point" text presents a number of statements about bullying. Based on these statements, what is the "Point" author's opinion about schools' effectiveness in reducing bullying? What is the author's purpose for writing?

2. The introductory three paragraphs of the "Counterpoint" text focus on events at a specific school. Based on the example of this school, what is the "Counterpoint" author's opinion about schools' effectiveness in reducing bullying? What is the author's purpose for writing? Highlight evidence from the text and make annotations to explain your response.

3. Identify one claim or reason that the "Counterpoint" author makes within paragraphs 4 through 9 that is well-supported by evidence. Highlight textual evidence and make annotations to explain your analysis.

4. Identify one claim or reason that the "Point" author makes within paragraphs 4 through 6 that is not well-supported by evidence. Highlight evidence from the text and make annotations to support your analysis.

5. Based on the ideas presented in both articles, how are schools dealing with the challenges of bullying? In what ways are schools standing up or failing to stand up for the victims of bullying? Highlight textual evidence and make annotations to explain your ideas.

WRITING PROMPT

The "Point" and "Counterpoint" authors offer two points of view on whether schools are doing enough to prevent bullying. Both offer reasons and evidence to support their claims. If you trace and evaluate the argument and specific claim of each author, which author is most convincing? Which author most effectively uses reasons and evidence to support his or her claim? Does one author cite more credible sources? Use your understanding of purpose and point of view as you evaluate the argument in each passage. Support your own argument and claim with relevant and well-organized evidence from the texts.

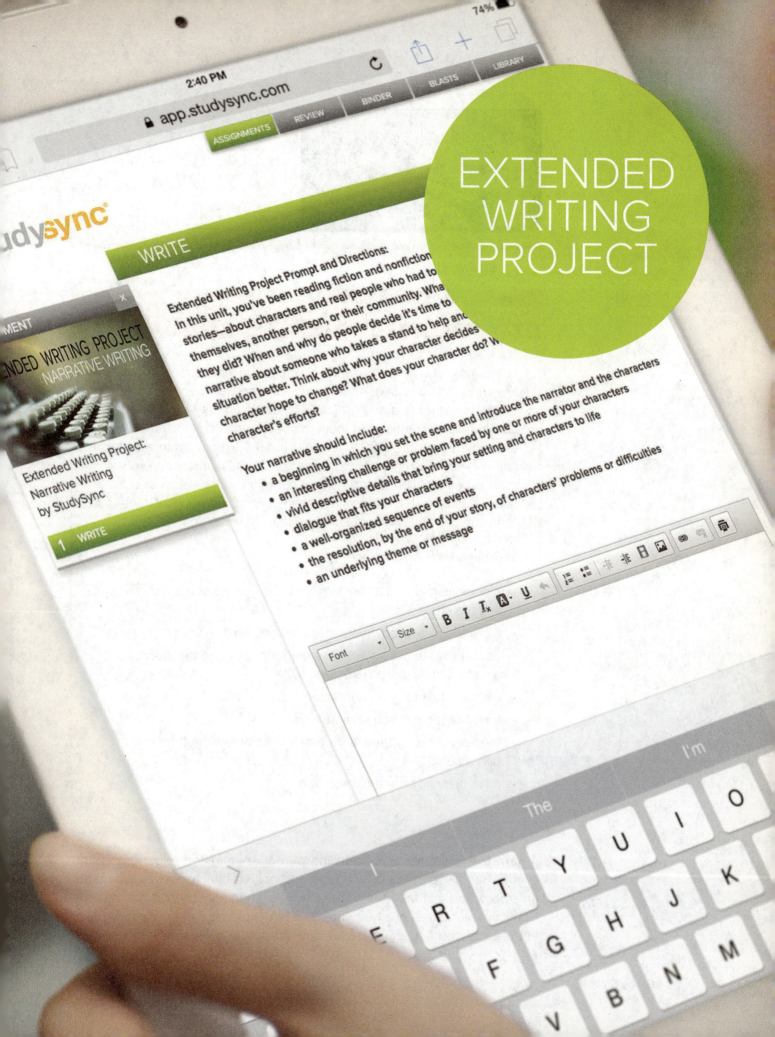

STUDYSYNC LIBRARY | Extended Writing Project

NARRATIVE WRITING

WRITING PROMPT

In this unit, you've been reading fiction and nonfiction narratives—imagined and true stories—about characters and real people who had to choose whether to stand up for themselves, another person, or their community. What motivated them to speak and act as they did? When and why do people decide it's time to take action? Write a fictional narrative about someone who takes a stand to help another person or to make a bad situation better. Think about why your character decides to take a stand. What does your character hope to change? What does your character do? What is the outcome of your character's efforts?

Your narrative should include:

- a beginning in which you set the scene and introduce the narrator and the characters
- a challenge or problem faced by one or more of your characters
- descriptive details and precise language to bring the story's events, setting, and characters to life
- dialogue that fits your characters
- a well-organized sequence of events
- the resolution, by the story's end, of characters' problems or difficulties
- an underlying theme or message

A **narrative** is the telling or retelling of real or imagined experiences and events. Narratives can be fiction or nonfiction. Fictional narratives are made-up stories and can take the form of novels, short stories, poems, or plays. Nonfiction narratives are true stories, often expressed in memoirs or diary entries, personal essays or letters, autobiographies or biographies, eyewitness accounts or histories. Many narratives have a clearly identified narrator who tells the story as it unfolds. In nonfiction narratives, the author usually tells the story. In fictional narratives, the narrator can be a character in the story or someone outside the story. Effective fictional narratives generally focus on a problem or conflict that needs to be resolved. The writer uses storytelling techniques such as dialogue, pacing, and description to develop events and characters. Events are generally presented in sequence, and transition words are used as needed to clarify time order.

The features of narrative writing include:

- setting—the time and place in which your story happens
- characters or real individuals
- plot—the sequence of events in a story
- point of view—the narrator's perspective on people and events
- precise language and descriptive details
- theme—the message about life that a story communicates

As you actively participate in this Extended Writing Project, you will receive more instructions and practice to help you craft each of the elements of narrative writing

STUDENT MODEL

Before you begin to write your own fictional narrative (or story), begin by reading this story that one student wrote in response to the writing prompt. As you read this Student Model, highlight and annotate the features of narrative writing that the student included in his or her fictional narrative.

Taking the Shot

I wanted to scream every time I saw it happening. My brother Kyle would get handed a basketball during gym class. He would dutifully stand in front of the net, try to line up his shot, and then wildly hurl the ball, which almost always landed in an entirely different part of the gym. Sometimes it bounced into the bleachers, catching bystanders by surprise. Sometimes it rolled into the girls' changing room. One time, it got stuck in an air vent. Then the teasing would begin. The minute the coach turned his back, the trio of mean boys would start laughing and talking trash. They'd say stuff like "Take cover, guys; Kyle is chucking the ball again. Your height is totally wasted on you, man. Your twin sister Celia has got all the athletic talent in your family, dude."

Then Kyle would shrug and say something like, "Yep. She's a great ball player. But I'm a great cook," and walk off the court.

He's right. He's a great cook! He takes after my dad, who's the head chef at the Pasta Pot. Kyle even made ribs for the whole family last week—with just a little help from my dad. And Kyle's good at other things, too—especially science. He says chemistry is like cooking with another name.

So, he can't throw a ball. Who cares? I wanted those guys to quit teasing him. It made me bonkers to see Kyle just give up and walk off the court, while those horrible kids made fun of him!

One day, when we were standing in the kitchen at our house, I asked him about it. I said, "Why don't you let me teach you how to do a free throw, so those guys will leave you alone?"

He said, "Celia, those guys don't bother me. Why do they bother you?"

Good question. Why do kids like that make me go bananas? Because they pick on the kids whose talents they don't recognize. Because it makes them feel big to say mean things about other people. That's not fair. I don't like it when things aren't fair. And that's what I told Kyle. But he just looked at me and went back to stirring a batch of vegetable soup. Sometimes I worry he'll mix-up our dinner with a science experiment, but that hasn't happened yet.

Now, here's a question my twin didn't ask me: *Why don't I stand up to those guys if I care so much?* My best friend, Mac, asked me that when we were playing basketball in the driveway.

"What do you mean?" I demanded.

Mac asked, "Are you afraid of those guys? Is that why you won't stand up for Kyle?"

I snatched the ball away from him and started dribbling. "No," I snapped. I was getting pretty angry myself. "Why would I be afraid of those guys?"

"Because they <u>are</u> mean. Because you <u>are</u> the only girl on the school basketball team. Because they could easily make you a target of their nasty comments, which would hurt. That's why."

Stunned, I tossed the ball and blew the shot. The ball bounced off the edge of the hoop with a metallic bang and into the garage. I knew that Mac was right. I was wrong. It was time to fix things. "All right," I said. "But I'm gonna need your help."

That weekend, Mac came over to our house with a new video game. It was one of those virtual sports games—basketball. Mac told Kyle that he was having trouble figuring it out. So Kyle, who is also great with computers, helped Mac set up the game. Then Mac showed Kyle how to toss a virtual basketball into a virtual hoop. Turns out, Kyle was actually very good. It seems that when Kyle isn't holding a real ball in his hands, he can line up a shot and make it. He and Mac spent all afternoon playing the computer game. I stayed out of the way.

So, the next time Kyle had to play basketball in gym class, we were both prepared, although Kyle didn't know it. He took the ball from the gym teacher and then stopped to calculate his shot—something he had learned from the video game. When he threw the ball, for the first time ever, it went toward the net. It actually bounced off the metal hoop! I could see that everyone—including the meanest boy of all—was amazed. But it wasn't like the gang suddenly turned nice or anything. "Missed again," one of them—a boy named Trey—hissed just loud enough for Kyle to hear.

I walked right up to Trey. "Give my brother a break," I shouted. That shocked the group for a couple of seconds. "He made a good shot. Deal with it.

"And besides," I told Trey in a quieter voice, "You're not so hot in science, you know. How would you feel if every time you answered a question, I yelled 'wrong!'"

He stared at me like I threw him for a loop. "Mr. Simon would never let you do that," he snarled.

By now, Kyle was tugging on my arm. "Come on," he said. "Let's just get out of here."

"True," I said to Trey. "He wouldn't. But Mr. Simon did say that my brother could help prep anybody who was failing science for the test next week. He thought it would be an okay thing to do during study hall. And aren't you kind of...well...having some trouble?"

Trey shot us a dirty look and walked away. "I don't need help," he barked. "Not from a loser."

What can you do? Without another word, we began heading out the door. Then, to our shock, another one of the mean boys, George, stopped us.

"Hey," George said.

"Hey," we answered.

"I could use a little help," George said.

I could tell he was shy about asking, because he wouldn't look at us. He just kept dribbling around us in circles. But before Kyle could say yes or no, George added "Help get me ready for the test, and afterwards I'll coach you, get you up to speed in the game."

I have to admit at that second, I felt kind of envious. I wouldn't have minded some extra coaching. I love basketball, and I'm good at it. And George is a super player.

On the other hand, Kyle is Kyle. He's just himself. He paused, and I could see him thinking over the offer. I knew he didn't want to reject George's temporary kindness. After all, maybe it would turn out to be more than temporary.

"I'll tell you what," Kyle said. "Basketball on a court isn't really my thing. But basketball on a computer…"

"…is a great game," George said, finishing Kyle's sentence. "I'd do that. Maybe this Sunday afternoon?"

I sighed with relief. Standing up for my brother was both easier and harder than I thought it would be. I made a plan and took a risk and it paid off. Phew! Now I could get back to the really important things in life—winning at basketball.

THINK QUESTIONS

1. What is the setting of the story in the first four paragraphs? Cite specific descriptive details that tell you when and where the events in the first four paragraphs of the story take place.

2. Who is the story's narrator, and how do you know? What other major character is introduced at the beginning of the story? What can you infer about both of these characters from the details in the first four paragraphs?

3. What happens in the story? Use time-order (or sequence) words to summarize the sequence of key events in the plot of the Student Model.

4. Think about the writing prompt. Which ideas from selections or other resources can be used as inspiration or models for your own narrative writing? For example, which authors of fiction or nonfiction narrative texts, in your opinion, use vivid, interesting language especially effectively or handle descriptive details particularly successfully? Which selections develop events in a sequence that unfolds in a very natural or interesting way? Support your ideas with evidence from the texts you have read.

5. Based on what you have read, listened to, or researched, how would you answer the question, "How do people decide when to stand up for themselves or on behalf of others?" What are some ways that people or characters respond when they or someone they love needs help or support? Cite details from the selections you have read so far in the unit.

STUDYSYNC LIBRARY | **Extended Writing Project**

NOTES

PREWRITE

WRITING PROMPT

In this unit, you've been reading fiction and nonfiction narratives—imagined and true stories—about characters and real people who had to choose whether to stand up for themselves, another person, or their community. What motivated them to speak and act as they did? When and why do people decide it's time to take action? Write a fictional narrative about someone who takes a stand to help another person or to make a bad situation better. Think about why your character decides to take a stand. What does your character hope to change? What does your character do? What is the outcome of your character's efforts?

Your narrative should include:

- a beginning in which you set the scene and introduce the narrator and the characters
- a challenge or problem faced by one or more of your characters
- descriptive details and precise language to bring the story's events, setting, and characters to life
- dialogue that fits your characters
- a well-organized sequence of events
- the resolution, by the story's end, of characters' problems or difficulties
- an underlying theme or message

In addition to studying the techniques authors use to tell stories, you have been reading real and imagined stories about individuals or characters who took a risk in deciding to stand up for themselves or others. In the Extended Writing Project, you will use those storytelling techniques to compose your own made-up narrative, or story.

NOTES

Because your story will be about characters who make choices about standing up for themselves or others, you will want to think about the characters or individuals you have read about in the unit texts. Think back to when you read the excerpt from *A Wrinkle in Time*: In what situation do Charles Wallace and Meg find themselves? What choices do the characters have? How do they ultimately respond to the strange man with the red eyes? How is Charles Wallace's reaction different from Meg's? How might a different character have acted?

Then consider how at least two other individuals or characters you have read about in this unit—for example, Ji-Li Jiang in *Red Scarf Girl* and Cassie and Stacey in *Roll of Thunder, Hear My Cry*—react when their families are in a tough situation. Think about similarities and differences that can help you as you begin to develop the characters, plot events—including the conflict (or problem)—and theme in your story. Think about who is telling your story and how involved he or she is.

Use the selections you have read as inspiration for getting started with a prewriting brainstorm activity to generate ideas for your own fictional narrative.

When you prewrite, you begin to develop ideas for your story, and you jot them down as they occur to you. What's important when you're prewriting is that you begin to generate ideas for your story, and that you begin to get excited about your ideas.

Remember, you're writing your story in response to the writing prompt shown at the top of this lesson. Review the writing prompt. Then, read the following list of questions to guide you in developing ideas for your story. Brainstorm and write answers to each of the questions. When you've answered all of the questions to your satisfaction, you've completed your prewriting brainstorm.

- Who are your characters?
- Who is telling the story?
- In what situation do your characters find themselves?
- What risks do your characters face if they stand up for themselves—and if they don't?
- What choices do your characters make?
- How will you organize your story's events?
- How does your story end?

STUDYSYNC LIBRARY | Extended Writing Project

SKILL: ORGANIZE NARRATIVE WRITING

DEFINE

The purpose of writing a narrative is to entertain readers while also guiding them to think about an important theme (or message)—a larger lesson about life or human experience. To convey the theme of a story, writers need to consider how to structure the story and organize the events in a way that makes sense.

Experienced writers carefully choose a **narrative text structure** that best suits their story. Most narratives use chronological (or sequential) text structure. To put it in simpler terms, this organization of a text is also called time order. It means that an author (or narrator) tells the events in the order in which they happen in a story. By telling what happens first, second, third, and so on, the author is giving the sequence of events. Along the way, this text structure enables the author to establish the setting, the narrator and characters, and the conflict (or problem) of the plot. Telling the events in time order also allows the characters and the action of the plot to move forward, through the middle of the story, when the main character (or characters) will attempt to resolve the conflict, or solve the problem. Finally, the story ends with the resolution of the conflict.

Sometimes instead of moving the plot forward in time and action, the plot moves the action backward in time, or even starts the action in the middle of the story. For example, if the story is character-driven, the plot might focus on the character's internal thoughts and feelings, so the writer might begin with a flashback to establish the character's issues or situation before moving into the present time. Similarly, if the story is a mystery, the writer might start the story in the middle to build suspense by making readers question why the person was murdered, for example, and "who done it."

To organize their story, writers often use a sequence-of-events chart, a timeline, or a flow chart. This type of graphic organizer will help them visualize and plot the order of events.

IDENTIFICATION AND APPLICATION

- The text structure for most narratives is sequential or chronological. However, a sequential text structure does not always mean that events are told in the exact order in which they happen. A writer might consider the following questions:
    > Should I tell the story in the order that the events happen?
    > Should I use a flashback at the beginning or start in the middle to create mystery and suspense?
    > Who are my characters and how will they grow or change?
    > What will be the most exciting moment of my story?
    > How will my story end?

- Although most stories are told in time order, writers may want to organize individual paragraphs by using a second kind of text structure:
    > For example, when a plot event leads to serious consequences for a character, the writer may use cause-and-effect text structure in the paragraph or paragraphs that tell about them.
    > A writer may use comparison-contrast text structure to tell how one character's reaction to an event was similar to or different from another's.
    > Despite these paragraph shifts in text structure (or organizational pattern) the overall structure for the story is still time order.

- Writers often use transition words and phrases to hint at the narrative's overall organization and the structure of individual sections or paragraphs:
    > Time order: *first, next, then, finally, before, after, now, soon,* in the meantime
    > Cause-effect: *because, so, therefore, as a result*
    > Compare-contrast: *like, similarly, in the same way* to compare and *although, while, but, however, on the other hand* to contrast
    > Order of importance: *mainly, most important, to begin with, first*

- In a chronological text structure, transition words and phrases also are used to signal shifts within the narrative in time and setting. Time order words and phrases are especially useful in indicating the sequence of events in a plot.

- The sequence of events in a narrative helps shape how a reader responds to what happens, and it also contributes to the overall development of the story's plot from beginning to end. You will learn more about narrative sequencing, and the elements and techniques that move the plot forward, in a later lesson.

MODEL

The writer of the Student Model understood from his or her prewriting that he or she would be telling the story in chronological order. In other words, the story would start at the beginning with the first event and end with the last event. In the first paragraph of the Model, the writer makes the organizational structure clear. The narrator, who is also a character in the story named Celia, tells about a series of events that often took place during gym class. She tells them in the order they happened. By using a mixture of the past tense (*wanted, landed, bounced, rolled*) and the past tense with the word would (*would get handed, would dutifully stand, would begin*) the narrator signals that she is telling about events that happened on an ongoing basis in the past. She also uses phrases such as "every time," and "almost always" to indicate that the events described in the opening paragraph were repeated more than once.

> I wanted to scream every time I saw it happening. My brother Kyle would get handed a basketball during gym class. He would dutifully stand in front of the net, try to line up his shot, and then wildly hurl the ball, which almost always landed in an entirely different part of the gym. Sometimes it bounced into the bleachers, catching bystanders by surprise. Sometimes it rolled into the girls' changing room. One time, it got stuck in an air vent. Then the teasing would begin. The minute the coach turned his back, the trio of mean boys would start laughing and talking trash. They'd say stuff like "Take cover, guys; Kyle is chucking the ball again. Your height is totally wasted on you, man. Your twin sister Celia has got all the athletic talent in your family, dude."

The writer of the Student Model uses time-order words and phrases such as "then" and "One time" to indicate **when** events happen. If changes in time are also accompanied by changes in place, the writer is careful to indicate **where** events happen, too. The first four paragraphs are set in the gym during the school day. The fifth and sixth paragraphs take place elsewhere:

> One day, when we were standing in the kitchen at our house, I asked him about it. I said, "Why don't you let me teach you how to do a free throw, so those guys will leave you alone?" He said, "Celia, those guys don't bother me. Why do they bother you?"

Throughout the story, the writer provides words and phrases that tell readers when and where the story's events are happening: "when we were playing basketball in the driveway," "that weekend," and "so, the next time Kyle had to play basketball in gym class."

In order to organize the order of the story's events, the writer used an Organize Narrative Writing Timeline. He or she listed the events and then numbered them in the order in which they would appear in the story. If the place changed, the writer noted that as well.

Event #1: Kyle always throws the basketball badly in gym class, and the mean boys tease him.
Event #2: Celia offers to teach Kyle how to throw a basketball, but Kyle declines.
Event #3: One day, Mac asks Celia when they're playing basketball in the driveway why she is too afraid of the mean boys to stand up for her brother.
Event #4: Mac gives her some good reasons, and Celia decides to make a plan to help her brother.
Event #5: That weekend, Mac comes over to the house with a video game and asks Kyle to show him how it works.
Event #6: Kyle helps set up the game and learns how to throw a basketball well.
Event #7: Kyle gets another chance to throw a basketball in gym class. He almost makes the shot.
Event #8: The mean boys tease Kyle anyway.
Event #9: Celia shouts at the boys. She says she doesn't tease them when they make mistakes in science class. She says Kyle could help them on the upcoming science test.
Event #10: Trey storms off, but George asks for help. He and Kyle might become friends.

PRACTICE

By using an Organize Narrative Writing timeline, you'll be able to fill in the events for your story that you began to consider during the prewriting stage of your Extended Writing Project. When you have completed your organizer, trade with a partner and offer each other feedback on the structure of events the writer has planned, and the use of transitions to make shifts in time order and setting clear for the reader.

STUDYSYNC LIBRARY | Extended Writing Project

SKILL: DESCRIPTIVE DETAILS

DEFINE

One way a writer develops the setting, characters, and plot in a narrative is by using description and descriptive details. In a story, the descriptive details help readers imagine the world in which the story takes place and the characters who live in it.

Descriptive details often use precise language—specific nouns and action verbs—to convey experiences or events. Many descriptive details use sensory language to appeal to one or more of the reader's five senses. Sensory words tell how something looks, sounds, feels, smells, or tastes.

Descriptive details should be relevant to the story, such as a character's actions or the setting. In a story, it is easy to include many interesting details, but not every detail is relevant. For example, what a character smells might be less relevant than how he or she feels or what he or she sees or hears during a key moment in the story. Too many details can make the reader feel overwhelmed. Plus, they can slow the pace of a story. It's a good idea to select only the most important, or relevant, details for your story. Think about what the reader really needs to know in order to understand or picture what is happening. Consider what your narrator actually knows and can share with the reader, especially if he or she is a character in the story. Then choose the details that will most help the readers imagine what the setting looks like, what the characters are experiencing, or how the events are happening.

IDENTIFICATION AND APPLICATION

- Description and descriptive details help a reader understand story elements such as:
  › characters (how they look, what they are wearing, what emotions their facial expressions reveal, what they are thinking versus what they say, what they do and how they behave)
  › setting (time, location, appearance of the place, atmosphere)

> conflict (the severity of the problem, whether the problem is getting better or worse)

- Authors use specific nouns and strong verbs, adjectives and adverbs as appropriate, to help create vivid details
- Sensory details in a narrative appeal to readers' five senses. They help draw a reader into a story and create an engaging experience.
- Figurative language such as similes and metaphors can enhance description of what the characters are seeing, experiencing, or feeling
- Description and descriptive details can help an author build the point of view or tone of the story.

MODEL

In the following excerpt from the Student Model, the writer has the narrator use vivid, precise language and specific details to describe her brother's experience in gym class. Think about how the words and details add to your understanding of the story.

> I wanted to scream every time I saw it happening. My brother Kyle would get handed a basketball during gym class. He would dutifully stand in front of the net, try to line up his shot, and then wildly hurl the ball, which almost always landed in an entirely different part of the gym. Sometimes it bounced into the bleachers, catching bystanders by surprise. Sometimes it rolled into the girls' changing room. One time, it got stuck in an air vent. Then the teasing would begin. The minute the coach turned his back, the trio of mean boys would start laughing and talking trash. They'd say stuff like "Take cover, guys; Kyle is chucking the ball again. Your height is totally wasted on you, man. Your twin sister Celia has got all the athletic talent in your family, dude."

The paragraph uses sports terminology ("line up his shot"), active verbs (*hurl, landed, bounced, chucking*), and specific nouns (*bleachers, bystanders, trio*) to describe what happens when Kyle tries to toss a basketball in gym class. Are all the details relevant? Do any of the details distract you from the scene or do they all help create a picture of Kyle and the mean boys?

One way to generate description and descriptive details is to use a graphic organizer. It can help you choose the most relevant descriptive details about your setting, characters, and plot events. Read the excerpt from the student model, "Taking the Shot." Then look at the organizer.

Now, here's a question my twin didn't ask me: *Why don't I stand up to those guys if I care so much?* My best friend, Mac, asked me that when we were playing basketball in the driveway.

"What do you mean?" I demanded.

Mac asked, "Are you afraid of those guys? Is that why you won't stand up for Kyle?"

I snatched the ball away from him and started dribbling. "No," I snapped. I was getting pretty angry myself. "Why would I be afraid of those guys?"

"Because they <u>are</u> mean. Because you <u>are</u> the only girl on the school basketball team. Because they could easily make you a target of their nasty comments, which would hurt. That's why."

Stunned, I tossed the ball and blew the shot. The ball bounced off the edge of the hoop with a metallic bang and into the garage. I knew that Mac was right. I was wrong. It was time to fix things. "All right," I said. "But I'm gonna need your help."

DESCRIPTIVE DETAILS	
Precise words and phrases	**Stunned,** I **tossed** the ball and **blew** the shot. The ball **bounced** off the edge of the hoop with a metallic bang and into the garage. [This language is precise. It uses sports terms and active verbs.]
Relevant descriptive details	"No," I snapped. **I was getting pretty angry myself.** "Why would I be afraid of those guys?" [This detail is relevant. It reveals what the character is feeling.]
Sensory language	**I snatched the ball away** from him and started dribbling. [This detail appeals to one's sense of touch.]

As the writer planned the Student Model, he or she asked some questions to determine which descriptive details would be the most relevant:

- Will this detail help the reader understand who the character is, and why he or she thinks, says, feels, or acts a certain way?
- Will this detail help the reader understand what the character is experiencing?
- Does this detail use language that is interesting and will appeal to one or more of the reader's five senses?
- Will this detail add to the story and help it move forward, or will it slow down the pace of the story?

PRACTICE

Use a Descriptive Details graphic organizer like the one in the model to create some descriptive details for your story that appeal to the senses. Then trade your details with a partner when you are finished. Offer feedback about the details. Engage in a peer review to determine which details are strong enough to help readers visualize your setting, understand your characters, follow events, and remember your message.

PLAN

WRITING PROMPT

In this unit, you've been reading fiction and nonfiction narratives—imagined and true stories—about characters and real people who had to choose whether to stand up for themselves, another person, or their community. What motivated them to speak and act as they did? When and why do people decide it's time to take action? Write a fictional narrative about someone who takes a stand to help another person or to make a bad situation better. Think about why your character decides to take a stand. What does your character hope to change? What does your character do? What is the outcome of your character's efforts?

Your narrative should include:

- a beginning in which you set the scene and introduce the narrator and the characters
- a challenge or problem faced by one or more of your characters
- descriptive details and precise language to bring the story's events, setting, and characters to life
- dialogue that fits your characters
- a well-organized sequence of events
- the resolution, by the story's end, of characters' problems or difficulties
- an underlying theme or message

Review the ideas you brainstormed in the prewrite activity and then take another look at the events you listed in your *Organize Narrative Writing* Graphic Organizer and at the details you listed on your *Descriptive Details Graphic* Organizer. Think about what you have learned about audience and purpose and about creating details to develop your setting and characters.

Remember all the stories you have read. A story's plot has a beginning, middle, and end. These ideas will help you create a Story Road Map to use for writing your story.

Consider the following questions as you develop the Road Map for your narrative:

- Where and when does your story take place?
- Who are your characters? What are they like?
- Who is telling your story? Is the narrator a character in the story? Or is the narrator telling the story from outside the text?
- What challenge or problem do your characters face?
- How do your characters deal with the challenge, or problem? Do they stand up for themselves or for someone else?
- How do your characters grow or change as the story moves forward?
- What is the most exciting moment in your story?
- What happens to your characters at the end?
- What theme (or message) do you want your readers to take away from your story?

This Story Road Map has been completed with details from the Student Model, "Taking the Shot." Use it as a model for creating a Road Map for your own story.

STUDYSYNC LIBRARY | Extended Writing Project

Story Road Map

Character(s):

Characters: Celia (the narrator), Kyle (Celia's twin brother), Mac, the three mean boys. Kyle is bad at basketball but great at other things—cooking, school. Celia cares about him a lot!

Setting(s):

Middle school gymnasium, Celia and Kyle's house and driveway

Beginning:

Celia tells about how her brother Kyle gets teased by three mean boys when he can't throw a basketball properly during gym class.

Middle:

At home, Celia offers to teach Kyle how to throw a basketball, but he declines. Mac asks Celia why she is upset by the mean boys. She figures out that she is actually kind of afraid of them herself. She makes a plan with Mac to help Kyle. Mac brings over a video game. By playing it, Kyle learns some tips for throwing a basketball.

End:

Back in gym class, Kyle does better at basketball, but the mean boys tease him anyway. Celia yells at them and tells them that she doesn't tease the boys when they make mistakes in science class. She says that Kyle can tutor them. The boy named Trey refuses, but George accepts the offer. He and Kyle might become friends.

STUDYSYNC LIBRARY | Extended Writing Project

SKILL: INTRODUCTION/ STORY BEGINNING

DEFINE

The beginning of a fictional narrative is the opening passage in which the writer provides the exposition, or the important details about the story's setting, narrator, characters, plot, conflict, and even the theme. A strong introduction captures the attention of readers, making them want to read on to find out what happens next.

IDENTIFICATION AND APPLICATION

- The beginning of a narrative (or story) includes **exposition**. The exposition establishes the setting, the characters, the narrator, the narrator's point of view, the plot, and even the theme. As in other forms of writing, writers use a "hook" to grab readers' interest. In a narrative, a hook can be an exciting moment, a detailed description, or a surprising or thoughtful comment made by the narrator or the main character.
- The beginning of a narrative also establishes the **structure** of the story. Remember: a story does not have to open with the start of the action. It can begin in the middle. This strategy "grabs" the reader's attention and builds suspense by making the reader wonder what's going on. Some stories even begin at the end and work their way backward in time. These strategies use flashbacks to capture the reader's attention, but they are not necessary. Most good stories start at the beginning of the action and tell the events in time order. They use descriptive supporting details, engaging characters, and unexpected plot twists to keep readers interested.
- The beginning of a story might also offer clues about the **theme**. The theme is the message or "big idea" about life that the writer wants readers to understand. The theme is developed over the course of the story as the characters grow, change, and make decisions about life. Good writers drop hints at the beginning of the story so that readers can consider the "big idea" as they read.

- Many features of a narrative, including some aspects of the introduction, are the same in fiction and nonfiction. You have already read that writers use a "hook" in the beginning of both types of narrative in order to engage readers' attention. In the beginning of a nonfiction narrative, readers usually also learn who the narrator is, when and where the narrative takes place, what the text structure will be (usually sequential), and what the narrative generally will be about.

MODEL

Reread the introduction to the excerpt from *Red Scarf Girl: A Memoir of the Cultural Revolution* by Ji-Li Jiang. The narrative is nonfiction, but the opening section of this excerpt includes a hook designed to capture readers' attention: the words "Don't be afraid." As soon as readers hear a phrase like that, they know they will be reading about something a little scary.

> "Sit down, sit down. Don't be afraid." Chairman Jin pointed to the empty chair. "These comrades from your father's work unit are just here to have a study session with you. It's nothing to worry about."
>
> I sat down dumbly.
>
> I had thought about their coming to my home but never imagined this. They were going to expose my family in front of my teachers and classmates. I would have no pride left. I would never be an educable child again.
>
> Thin-Face sat opposite me, with a woman I had never seen before. Teacher Zhang was there too, his eyes encouraging me.
>
> Thin-Face came straight to the point. "Your father's problems are very serious. " His cold eyes nailed me to my seat.

Ji-Li herself is the narrator and the central figure in this narrative, which tells part of her real-life story. Her use of first-person pronouns tells the reader that events will be recounted from her perspective or point of view. This section of the narrative introduces not only the narrator but also other important individuals in the story, along with the disturbing situation Ji-Li faces. Chairman Jin's words, "Don't be afraid," instantly create a feeling of danger. The problem Ji-Li experiences in the narrative is clear—her family is about to be "exposed" in front of her teachers and classmates. Her own pride will be destroyed by the accusations. Readers can infer what will happen next: she will have to choose between being considered an "educable child" and standing by her

STUDYSYNC LIBRARY | **Extended Writing Project**

family. From the start of the excerpt, readers can guess that one of the themes of the narrative will be about loyalty and betrayal.

Although Ji-Li does not provide a lot of details about the setting, she seems to be the only child in a room full of adults. The sense of a bleak setting accentuates a feeling of her powerlessness. She feels "nailed to her seat." The beginning of this excerpt sets up a tense and unpredictable situation.

PRACTICE

Write a beginning for your fictional story. It should introduce your setting, narrator, and main character (or characters), as well as the conflict (or problem) of the plot. Include a "hook" that will grab readers' attention.

STUDYSYNC LIBRARY | Extended Writing Project

SKILL: NARRATIVE TECHNIQUES AND SEQUENCING

 PLAN

When writing a story, authors use a variety of narrative techniques to develop both the plot and the characters, explore the setting, and engage the reader. These techniques include dialogue, a sequencing of events, pacing, and description. **Dialogue**, what the characters say to one another, is often used to develop characters and move the events of the plot forward. Every narrative contains a **sequence of events**, which is carefully planned and controlled by the author as the story unfolds. Writers often manipulate the **pacing** of a narrative, or the speed with which events occur, to slow down or speed up the action at certain points in a story. This can create tension and suspense. Writers use **description** to build story details and reveal information about the characters, setting, and plot.

The beginning of a story is called the **introduction** or **exposition**. This is the part of the story in which the writer provides the reader with essential information, introducing the characters, the time and place in which the action occurs, and the problem or conflict the characters must face and attempt to solve.

As the story continues, the writer includes details and events to develop the conflict and move the story forward. These events—known as the **rising action** of the story—build until the story reaches its **climax**. This is a turning point in the story, where the most exciting and intense action usually occurs. It is also the point at which the characters begin to find a solution to the problem or conflict in the plot.

The writer then focuses on details and events that make up the **falling action** of the story. This is everything that happens after the climax, leading to a **resolution.** These elements make up a story's **conclusion,** which often contains a message or final thought for the reader.

STUDYSYNC LIBRARY | Extended Writing Project

IDENTIFICATION AND APPLICATION

- Most narratives are written in sequential order. However, arranging events in time order is not the only skill involved in narrative sequencing. Writers group events to shape both a reader's response to what happens and the development of the plot from beginning to end.
  - *Exposition refers* to the essential information at the start of a story.
  - *Rising action* refers to the sequence of events leading up to a story's turning point.
    - The turning point is called the climax, and it's usually the most suspenseful moment in the story.
    - During the rising action, readers may experience anticipation, curiosity, concern, or excitement.
  - *Falling action* refers to the sequence of events following the story's turning point, or climax, and leading to the resolution of the story's conflict or problem.
    - During the falling action, readers may look forward to finding out how the story will end.

- Pacing is a technique writers use to control the speed with which events are revealed. Description and dialogue can help writers vary the pacing in a narrative.
- Description uses specific details, precise language, and sensory words to develop characters, setting, and events. It can be used to slow down pacing.
- Dialogue, or the exchange of words between two or more characters, can reveal character traits and important plot details. Dialogue can be used to speed up or slow down pacing. A short, snappy line of dialogue might speed up a story. A long speech might slow it down.
  - Dialogue is set in its own paragraph and inside quotation marks. A line of dialogue might look like this: "My name is Jeannette."
  - Dialogue is usually followed by a tag, such as *she said* or *he asked,* to indicate who is speaking.
  - Dialogue should suit the character who speaks it. Business executives at an important meeting would speak differently from teenagers playing a game at a friend's house.

MODEL

Following its introduction or beginning section, the Student Model develops the characters and events of the story, including the conflict (or problem) that the main character faces. In these paragraphs, the rising action moves the first-person narrator, Celia, to the point of recognizing that she has to stand up for her brother. The writer uses description and dialogue to enrich the story and to vary the pacing of events. Some paragraphs are longer than others. Some include dialogue, and some don't. Some include more descriptive details than others or different types of sentences. By varying the pacing, writers hold readers' interest.

Reread paragraphs 3-9 from the middle of the Student Model, "Taking the Shot." Look closely at the text structure and at the way in which the sequence of events consists of rising action that builds toward a change in Celia.

> He's right. He's a great cook! He takes after my dad, who's the head chef at the Pasta Pot. Kyle even made ribs for the whole family last week—with just a little help from my dad. And Kyle's good at other things, too—especially science. He says chemistry is like cooking with another name.
>
> So, he can't throw a ball. Who cares? I wanted those guys to quit teasing him. It made me bonkers to see Kyle just give up and walk off the court, while those horrible kids made fun of him!
>
> One day, when we were standing in the kitchen at our house, I asked him about it. I said, "Why don't you let me teach you how to do a free throw, so those guys will leave you alone?"
>
> He said, "Celia, those guys don't bother me. Why do they bother you?"
>
> Good question. Why do kids like that make me go bananas? Because they pick on the kids whose talents they don't recognize. Because it makes them feel big to say mean things about other people. That's not fair. I don't like it when things aren't fair. And that's what I told Kyle. But he just looked at me and went back to stirring a batch of vegetable soup. Sometimes I worry he'll mix-up our dinner with a science experiment, but that hasn't happened yet.
>
> Now, here's a question my twin didn't ask me: *Why don't I stand up to those guys if I care so much?* My best friend, Mac, asked me that when we were playing basketball in the driveway.
>
> "What do you mean?" I demanded.

Notice how the third paragraph of the story (the first paragraph above) focuses on one thing—details that tell what the character of Kyle is like. (The choice of details that Celia, the narrator, includes says something about her character, too.) The fourth paragraph of the story tells readers how the narrator feels. The fifth and sixth paragraphs of the story feature dialogue, or words spoken by the characters. The author places the words within quotation marks and uses tags, such as "I said" and "He said" to indicate who is speaking and to whom. Dialogue reveals directly what the characters are thinking. The short, conversational sentences also tend to speed up the pace of the story. Notice also the vivid descriptive detail in the seventh paragraph: "stirring a batch of vegetable soup."

Most important, notice what happens in the story. Celia offers to help her brother, but he turns down her offer. The action continues to rise toward a turning point when Max asks Celia a question that makes her realize she has her own reasons for not yet taking a stand.

PRACTICE

Write one paragraph of rising action for your narrative. Use your paragraph to develop an event that helps lead to your story's climax. Include elements such as dialogue, sensory language, and specific details. Be sure that the text structure of your paragraph is clear, and that transitions clarify any changes in time or setting. When you are finished, trade with a partner and offer each other feedback. Remember that comments are most helpful when they are constructive.

SKILL: CONCLUSION/ STORY ENDING

DEFINE

The **conclusion** is the final section of a narrative (or story). It is where the readers find out what happens to the characters. The plot winds down, and the main character's conflict (or problem) is resolved. The ending of a narrative is called the resolution. In some stories, the narrator or a character leaves readers with a final lesson about life or human experience. More often, however, readers have to figure out the lesson, or theme, on their own by drawing inferences from the end of the story.

IDENTIFICATION AND APPLICATION

- An effective ending brings the story to a satisfying close. It follows from the story's events, resolves the conflict, ties up loose ends, and may hint at what happens to the characters when the story is over.
  > The way a problem is resolved (the resolution) should be logical and feel like a natural part of the plot, but it can still be a surprise.
  > The resolution should tell clearly how the characters resolved the conflict (or problem)—or how it was resolved for them.
  > The concluding statement may sum up the story and leave readers feeling as if they were thoroughly entertained and thinking "That was a great story!"

- The conclusion might also include a memorable comment from the narrator or a character that helps readers understand the theme—the larger lesson about life or human experience that the story conveyed.

MODEL

In the conclusion to the nonfiction excerpt from *Red Scarf Girl: A Memoir of the Cultural Revolution,* the narrator Ji-Li Jiang is faced with a terrible choice.

A local Communist official has told Ji-Li that she must choose between defending her father, who the officials say betrayed the Communist Party, and continuing with her education and being accepted as a good Communist. Either way, Ji-Li will lose. What will she decide to do? Will she stand up for herself? Will she defend her father? Will she give in to the local officials' demands?

> "Now, you have to choose between two roads." Thin-Face looked straight into my eyes. "You can break with your family and follow Chairman Mao, or you can follow your father and become an enemy of the people." His voice grew more severe. "In that case we would have many more study sessions, with your brother and sister too, and the Red Guard Committee and the school leaders. Think about it. We will come back to talk to you again."
>
> Thin-Face and the woman left, saying they would be back to get my statement. Without knowing how I got there, I found myself in a narrow passageway between the school building and the school-yard wall. The gray concrete walls closed around me and a slow drizzle dampened my cheeks. I could not go back to the classroom, and I could not go home.

Ji-Li does not make her decision, but it is clear that her loyalties are torn and she is frightened. Readers can only guess at the decision that Ji-Li will make in the sections that follow. Is her father's love worth the risk? Can she help her family more if she agrees to condemn her father but can get her education? These struggles are what eventually will lead her to a resolution of her conflict or problem. As you have noticed in your own reading, very few real-life or made-up stories end with the characters in the middle of a conflict. The conflict or problem must be resolved in some way for the story to be satisfying for the reader.

Now, read this section from the last few paragraphs of the Student Model:

> "I'll tell you what," Kyle said. "Basketball on a court isn't really my thing. But basketball on a computer..."
>
> "...is a great game," George said, finishing Kyle's sentence. "I'd do that. Maybe this Sunday afternoon?"
>
> I sighed with relief.

With the resolution of Celia's conflict and Kyle's problem, the story is moving toward its conclusion. One of the mean boys has offered to become friendly with Kyle. Kyle remains true to himself while at the same time accepting George's offer of friendship. And Celia, who has at last bravely stood up for her brother, experiences a moment of relief that everything seems to be working out. The resolution is satisfying to main characters and to the reader as well.

The last sentences of the very last paragraph of the Student Model flow naturally from the story's events and ends on an amusing note:

> I made a plan and took a risk and it paid off. Phew! Now I could get back to the really important things in life—winning at basketball.

Write an ending for your fictional story. It should let your readers know how the main character (or characters) resolved the conflict (or problem). Your ending might also hint at what happens to the character after the story is over. In your conclusion (or ending), try to include a thoughtful statement about life or human experience. Your message might be something that the narrator or a character says, or it might be an inference about the theme that the reader can draw from specific evidence in the text.

STUDYSYNC LIBRARY | Extended Writing Project

NOTES

DRAFT

WRITING PROMPT

In this unit, you've been reading fiction and nonfiction narratives—imagined and true stories—about characters and real people who had to choose whether to stand up for themselves, another person, or their community. What motivated them to speak and act as they did? When and why do people decide it's time to take action? Write a fictional narrative about someone who takes a stand to help another person or to make a bad situation better. Think about why your character decides to take a stand. What does your character hope to change? What does your character do? What is the outcome of your character's efforts?

Your narrative should include:

- a beginning in which you set the scene and introduce the narrator and the characters
- a challenge or problem faced by one or more of your characters
- descriptive details and precise language to bring the story's events, setting, and characters to life
- dialogue that fits your characters
- a well-organized sequence of events
- the resolution, by the story's end, of characters' problems or difficulties
- an underlying theme or message

You've already made progress toward writing your own fictional narrative. You've thought about your characters and their conflict (or problem), setting, plot, and theme. You've considered your audience and purpose, determined an appropriate text structure to organize your ideas and events, and generated plenty of supporting details. You've practiced writing a beginning section and ending for your story. Now it's time to write a full draft of your story.

Use your timeline of events and other graphic organizers to help you as you write. Remember that a fictional narrative has an introduction, a middle, and a conclusion. The introduction (or beginning) establishes the setting, the narrator, the characters, and conflict (or problem) of the story. The middle section develops the characters and plot by using narrative techniques such as description, pacing, and dialogue. Transitions enable readers to follow the sequence of events by signalling changes in time or setting. Throughout the story, precise language—including specific nouns, strong verbs, and descriptive and sensory details—allows readers to picture the characters and events. The conclusion (or ending) tells how the characters resolve their problem, or how it is resolved for them. It ties up loose ends and hints at the theme of the story and its important message. An effective ending can also do more—it can leave a lasting impression on your readers.

When drafting your story, ask yourself these questions:

- How can I improve my introduction to "hook" my readers?
- Who is the narrator of my story?
- What relevant supporting details, description, and precise or sensory words can I add to fully develop the characters, experiences, and events in my story?
- Have I included dialogue that fits the characters?
- Have I ordered the events of the plot so that my body paragraphs move the characters and action forward? Have I varied the pacing of events to hold readers' interest?
- What transition words and phrases might make the order of events clearer?
- Is the end of my story interesting or surprising? Is the resolution of the conflict believable?
- Will my readers understand the theme? What changes can I make to present a clearer theme (or message) to my readers?
- Have I corrected errors in grammar, punctuation, and spelling?

Before you submit your draft, read it over carefully. You want to be sure that you have responded to all aspects of the prompt.

STUDYSYNC LIBRARY | **Extended Writing Project**

NOTES

REVISE

WRITING PROMPT

In this unit, you've been reading fiction and nonfiction narratives—imagined and true stories—about characters and real people who had to choose whether to stand up for themselves, another person, or their community. What motivated them to speak and act as they did? When and why do people decide it's time to take action? Write a fictional narrative about someone who takes a stand to help another person or to make a bad situation better. Think about why your character decides to take a stand. What does your character hope to change? What does your character do? What is the outcome of your character's efforts?

Your narrative should include:

- a beginning in which you set the scene and introduce the narrator and the characters
- a challenge or problem faced by one or more of your characters
- descriptive details and precise language to bring the story's events, setting, and characters to life
- dialogue that fits your characters
- a well-organized sequence of events
- the resolution, by the story's end, of characters' problems or difficulties
- an underlying theme or message

You have written a draft of your narrative. You have also received input and advice from your peers about how to improve it. Now you are going to revise your draft. Here are some recommendations to help you revise:

- Review the suggestions made by your peers.
- Focus on your use of transitions. Transitions are words or phrases that help your readers follow the flow of events and ideas.
  - As you revise, look for places where you can add transition words or phrases to help make the order of events or the relationship between ideas clearer. Do transition words indicate shifts in time and setting?
  - Test the transitions you have used or want to add. Make sure they reflect the relationship that you want to convey. Review the types of transition words you can use—chronological (sequential or time order), cause-effect, compare-contrast, problem-solution, spatial, order of importance, and so on.

- After you have revised your body paragraphs for transitions, think about whether there is anything else you can do to improve your introduction and conclusion.
  - Do you need a better "hook" at the beginning of your story to grab readers' interest?
  - Do you need to add or subtract details or events from the middle of your story? Does your story drag a little in the middle or does it skip over important details or events readers need to know?
  - Does your conclusion wrap up the story in a satisfying way? Or do you need to provide more details about what happens to the characters?
  - Does your conclusion leave readers with a message about life? Do you need to have a character or the narrator state this theme directly? Or can you add details that hint at the theme?

- As you revise, be aware of how you are using language to express characters' thoughts, words, and actions, along with the events that make up the narrative.
  - Are you varying the types of sentences you're using? Writing becomes boring when it sounds the same. Incorporating a variety of simple, compound, and complex sentences into your writing adds interest. Remember, a simple sentence has one subject and one predicate; a compound sentence contains two or more simple sentences joined by a comma and a coordinating conjunction (such as *and, but* or *or*) or by a semicolon. A complex sentence has an independent clause and one or more dependent clauses.
  - Are you choosing words carefully? Remember that in writing, less is often more. Look for ideas or sentences that you can combine or delete to avoid unnecessary repetition, and make your word choice as precise as it can be.

> Are you using a mixture of standard and conversational English? Use the language that best suits your narrator and characters, but also keep in mind that your readers need to be able to understand the writing or they will lose interest.
> Does your dialogue sound believable? Avoid using a lot of slang that readers won't know, but don't make your characters sound pretentious by using ornate language, or they won't sound believable.
> Are you using pronouns properly? If it is not clear to what or to whom your pronouns refer, your readers could get confused. Don't let small errors get in the way of telling an effective story.
> Are you you carefully checking your spelling and punctuation?

STUDYSYNC LIBRARY | Extended Writing Project

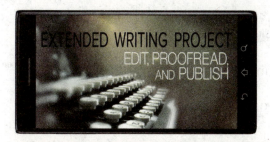

EDIT, PROOFREAD, AND PUBLISH

WRITING PROMPT

In this unit, you've been reading fiction and nonfiction narratives—imagined and true stories—about characters and real people who had to choose whether to stand up for themselves, another person, or their community. What motivated them to speak and act as they did? When and why do people decide it's time to take action? Write a fictional narrative about someone who takes a stand to help another person or to make a bad situation better. Think about why your character decides to take a stand. What does your character hope to change? What does your character do? What is the outcome of your character's efforts?

Your narrative should include:

- a beginning in which you set the scene and introduce the narrator and the characters
- a challenge or problem faced by one or more of your characters
- descriptive details and precise language to bring the story's events, setting, and characters to life
- dialogue that fits your characters
- a well-organized sequence of events
- the resolution, by the story's end, of characters' problems or difficulties
- an underlying theme or message

You have revised your narrative and received input from your peers on your revised writing. Now it's time to edit and proofread your story to produce a final version. Have you included all the valuable suggestions from your peers? Ask yourself: Have I effectively introduced and fully developed my setting, characters, plot, conflict (or problem), and theme? What more can I do to improve my story's supporting descriptive details? Did I use transitions well to move from event to event? Did I provide an engaging ending that follows from the story's events? Did I use varied sentence structure, realistic dialogue, and appropriate variations on standard English to make my writing more interesting?

When you are satisfied with your work, proofread it for errors. Use this list to check for correct:

- capitalization
- punctuation
- spelling
- grammar
- usage

In addition, check for correct punctuation in the dialogue, particularly for nonrestrictive elements. Check that you matched the number and gender of each pronoun to the person or thing it referred to; for example: *The dog wagged its tail at the arrival of its owner. Don checked for his smart phone, while Donna clutched her keys.*

Once you have made your corrections to your writing, you are ready to submit and publish your work. You can distribute your story to family and friends, attach it to a bulletin board, or post it to your blog. If you publish online, create links to the stories that have inspired you in this unit. That way, readers can read more stories that they might enjoy. Remember, too, that another way to have your story reach an audience is by becoming a storyteller. Tell your story to friends and classmates. Presenting a narrative orally can be fun both for the writer who created the story and for the audience who listens to it.

PHOTO/IMAGE CREDITS:

Cover, ©iStock.com/aijohn784, ©iStock.com/vernonwiley, ©iStock.com/alexey_boldin, ©iStock.com/skegbydave
p. v, ©iStock.com/DNY59, ©iStock.com/alexey_boldin, ©iStock.com/LaraBelova
p. vi, E+/Getty Images
p. vii, ©iStock.com/moevin, ©iStock.com/skegbydave, ©iStock.com/Chemlamp
p. 2, ©iStock.com/vernonwiley
p. 4, ©iStock.com/cemagraphics
p. 10, ©iStock.com/JordiDelgado
p. 17, ©iStock.com/hdtravelpix
p. 22, Hulton Archive/stringer/Getty Images
p. 27, ©iStock.com/JoeRosh
p. 33, Interim Archives/Getty Images
p. 38, ©iStock.com/Oleh_Pershyn
p. 46, ©iStock.com/AZemdega
p. 54, ©iStock.com/Mordolff
p. 58, ©iStock.com/SolStock
p. 65, ©iStock.com/moevin, ©iStock.com/svariophoto
p. 66, ©iStock.com/moevin, ©iStock.com/skegbydave
p. 72, ©iStock.com/moevin, ©iStock.com/skegbydave
p. 74, ©iStock.com/lcsdesign, ©iStock.com/skegbydave
p. 79, ©iStock.com/Jasmina007, ©iStock.com/skegbydave
p. 83, ©iStock.com/moevin, ©iStock.com/skegbydave
p. 86, ©iStock.com/bo1982, ©iStock.com/skegbydave
p. 89, ©iStock.com/fotokostic, ©iStock.com/skegbydave
p. 93, ©iStock.com/stevedangers, ©iStock.com/skegbydave
p. 96, ©iStock.com/moevin, ©iStock.com/skegbydave
p. 98, ©iStock.com/moevin, ©iStock.com/skegbydave
p. 101, ©iStock.com/moevin, ©iStock.com/skegbydave

Text Fulfillment Through StudySync

If you are interested in specific titles, please fill out the form below and we will check availability through our partners.

ORDER DETAILS

Date:

TITLE	AUTHOR	Paperback/Hardcover	Specific Edition *If Applicable*	Quantity

SHIPPING INFORMATION

Contact:
Title:
School/District:
Address Line 1:
Address Line 2:
Zip or Postal Code:
Phone:
Mobile:
Email:

BILLING INFORMATION ☐ SAME AS SHIPPING

Contact:
Title:
School/District:
Address Line 1:
Address Line 2:
Zip or Postal Code:
Phone:
Mobile:
Email:

PAYMENT INFORMATION

☐ CREDIT CARD

Name on Card:

Card Number: Expiration Date: Security Code:

☐ PO   Purchase Order Number:

StudySync Text Fulfillment, BookheadEd Learning, LLC
610 Daniel Young Drive | Sonoma, CA 95476